AQA Design and Technology

Textiles Technology

GCSE

Denise Davies

Amanda Dick

Liz Hardy

Nelson Thornes

Published in 2009 by:
Nelson Thornes Ltd
Delta Place
27 Bath Road
CHELTENHAM
GL53 7TH
United Kingdom

09 10 11 12 13 / 10 9 8 7 6 5 4 3 2

A catalogue record for this book is available from the British Library

ISBN 978 1 4085 0275 4

Cover photograph by Jim Wileman
Illustrations by Graham White/nb illustration and Fakenham Photosetting Ltd
Page make-up by Fakenham Photosetting Ltd
Printed and bound in Spain by GraphyCems

Acknowledgements

The authors and publishers wish to thank the following for permission to use copyright material:

p6 Daniel Oxtoby; p9 Jim Wileman; 1.1A, B iStockphoto, C Intertex; 1.2B Skoch3, C Aurora Silk, Portland, Oregon, D Public domain, E Australian Wool Innovation; 1.3A Science Photo Library, B, C Public domain, D iStockphoto, F Public domain, G Alamy; 1.4A Science Photo Library, B Thinking Of You, C iStockphoto, D Lyocell; 1.5A BHS Head Office, B Rex Features; 1.6A, B, C Graham White/nb illustration, D iStockphoto, iStockphoto, Next PLC, 1.7A iStockphoto, B Jason Newman; 1.8A, B Graham White/nb illustration; 1.9A iStockphoto; 1.10A Public domain; B www.enlighted.com, photography by Peter Rejcek, National Science Foundation, C Photo by Speedo; 2.1 Lutron Guide to Fabric specification reproduced with kind permission from Lutron www.lutron.com, B graces@btconnect.com, www.padoodles.com; 2.2A iStockphoto, C Jason Newman, D EEC; 2.3A Cheryl Kolander, B Public domain, C Cheryl Kolander, D Zhaoqing Fenglong Knitting Factory Co. Ltd, E iStockphoto, F The Style Council; 2.4A, B iStockphoto, C Alamy, Getty Images, Alamy; 3.1A Rabensteiner, B The Red Infirmary, C www.community.livejournal.com, D iStockphoto, E Nicholas Yarsley, F iStockphoto, G www.bill.net.au, H Nicholas Yarsley, I Alamy; 3.2B Nicholas Yarsley, p55 Daniel Oxtoby; 4.1D www.cjfold.com, E Daniel Oxtoby; 4.2B, C Getty, 4.3A Rex Features, B Samuel Manning; 4.4C www.crowdstorm.co.uk; 4.5C British Standards Institute; 4.6A Daniel Oxtoby, B Mothercare; 4.7A Corbis; 5.1A Topfoto, B O'Neill Europe, C Bagir Group, D Alibaba.com, F iStockphoto; 5.2A European Commission, The Fairtrade Foundation, B People Tree, www.peopletree.co.uk, C Topfoto, D www.blackyak.co.uk; 5.3A Public domain, B www.stylebubble.co.uk, D Nicholas Yarsley, F Luz Martin, www.junkystyling.co.uk; 5.4A Levi Strauss & Co., B The Soil Association, C Levi Strauss & Co., D Public Domain, E Ethical Fashion Designs by Feng Ho, photography by Alvaro Mari-Thompson; 5.5A Public domain, B www.rubyiris.com, D www.ecodesignz.nz, 5.6A www.hangcheongtoys.com, C Public domain, 6.1A Alamy, B iStockphoto, C Tex-Life, D Daniel Oxtoby, 6.2A Public domain, B Graham White/nb illustration; 6.3A Rex Features, B Copyright courtesy of Marks & Spencer PLC; 6.4B Graham White/nb illustration, C Daniel Oxtoby, D Getty Images, E Daniel Oxtoby, 6.5 A, B, C Graham White/nb illustration, D Public domain, E Nicholas Yarsley, F Graham White/nb illustration, G Evan Agostini/Getty Images, H Graham White/nb illustration; 6.6A Graham White/nb illustration, B Desert Deuce Surplus, C, D, E Graham White/nb illustration; 7.1B Getty Images; 7.2C www.surfshop-pau.com; 7.3B Topshop, Jill Stuart; 7.4A, B Getty Images, 8.1A Nicholas Yarsley, B Jason Newman; 8.2A Alamy, D Tootal; 8.3A www.Lectra.com; 9.1A Jupiter, B Alamy, C, D Samuel Manning; 9.2B, C Samuel Manning; 9.3B; 10.1A, B Samuel Manning; 10.2A, B Samuel Manning; 10.3A, B Samuel Manning; 10.4A, B Samuel Manning; 10.5A, B, C Samuel Manning; 10.6A, B, C Samuel Manning; 11.1A, B, Samuel Manning, C Daniel Oxtoby, D Daniel Oxtoby, E Samuel Manning; 11.3A Samuel Manning, Daniel Oxtoby, B Samuel Manning; 11.4A, B, C, D Samuel Manning, Daniel Oxtoby; 11.5A, B, C, D Samuel Manning; 11.6A, B Samuel Manning, C Jason Newman, D Daniel Oxtoby; 12.1A Samuel Manning, B Nicholas Yarsley; 12.2B, C Samuel Manning; 12.3A Nicholas Yarsley, B Samuel Manning.

Every effort has been made to contact the copyright holders and we apologise if any have been overlooked. Should copyright have been unwittingly infringed in this book, the owners should contact the publishers, who will make the corrections at reprint.

The controlled assessment tasks in this book are designed to help you prepare for the tasks your teacher will give you. The tasks in this book are not designed to test you formally and you cannot use them as your own controlled assessment tasks for AQA. Your teacher will not be able to give you as much help with your tasks for AQA as we have given with the tasks in this book.

Contents

Introduction   5

UNIT ONE

Written paper

Materials and components   8

Materials and components introduction   8

1 Fibres and fabrics   10

1.1   Choosing fibres and fabrics   10

1.2   Natural fibres and fabrics   12

1.3   Synthetic fibres and fabrics   14

1.4   Regenerated fibres and fabrics   18

1.5   Blended and mixed fibres   22

1.6   Fabric construction: woven   24

1.7   Fabric construction: non-woven   26

1.8   Fabric construction: knitted   28

1.9   Fabric finishes   30

1.10 The future of fibres and fabrics   32

2 Choice of fabric   34

2.1   Fabric choice and specification   34

2.2   Labelling   38

2.3   Dyeing and printing   40

2.4   Fabric enhancement   44

3 Components   46

3.1   Fastenings   46

3.2   Textile components   50

Materials and components examination-
style questions   52

Design and market influences   54

Design and market influences introduction   54

4 Product analysis and evaluation techniques   56

4.1   How designers get inspiration   56

4.2   Analysis of a product   60

4.3   Product disassembly   62

4.4   Evaluating design specifications   64

4.5   Quality assurance   66

4.6   Testing and evaluating design ideas   68

4.7   User trials and product comparison   70

5 Issues   72

5.1   Social and cultural influences   72

5.2   Moral issues   76

5.3   Recycling textiles   78

5.4   Environmental issues
      and sustainability   82

5.5   Health and safety: consumer rights   86

5.6   Health and safety: risk assessments   88

Design and market influences examination-
style questions   90

Processes and manufacture   92

Processes and manufacture introduction   92

6 Techniques and processes   94

6.1   Hand tools and equipment   94

6.2   Using machines in textile
      production   98

6.3   Production systems and processes   100

6.4   Techniques for product
      development   102

6.5   Construction techniques 1   106

6.6   Construction techniques 2   110

7 Production planning 112

7.1 Production flowcharts 112

7.2 Manufacturing specifications 114

7.3 Costing a product 116

7.4 Quality control 118

8 ICT 120

8.1 Use of ICT for researching and sorting information 120

8.2 Use of ICT to design and present 122

8.3 Use of ICT in manufacturing 126

Processes and manufacture examination-style questions 128

UNIT TWO

Controlled assessment task

Design and making practice 130

Design and making practice introduction 130

Your questions answered 131

9 Investigating the design opportunity 134

9.1 Analysis of the task 134

9.2 Research 136

9.3 Research analysis 138

10 Development of a design proposal 140

10.1 Design ideas 1 140

10.2 Design ideas 2 142

10.3 Planning the development of design ideas 144

10.4 Development of shape and style 146

10.5 Development of colour and decoration 148

10.6 Fabric and component choice 150

11 Making 152

11.1 The level of demand 152

11.2 Evidence in folders 156

11.3 Making skills 158

11.4 Making textile products 160

11.5 Inspirational made outcomes 162

11.6 Using modern technology 164

12 Testing and evaluation 166

12.1 Testing and evaluating throughout the task 166

12.2 Using specifications and consumers to test and evaluate 168

12.3 Final evaluation product analysis reports 170

Glossary 172

Index 175

Nelson Thornes has worked in partnership with AQA to ensure this book and the accompanying online resources offer you the best support for your GCSE course.

All resources have been approved by senior AQA examiners so you can feel assured that they closely match the specification for this subject and provide you with everything you need to prepare successfully for your exams.

These print and online resources together **unlock blended learning**; this means that the links between the activities in the book and the activities online blend together to maximise your understanding of a topic and help you achieve your potential.

These online resources are available on kerboodle! which can be accessed via the internet at **www.kerboodle.com/live**, anytime, anywhere. If your school or college subscribes to kerboodle! you will be provided with your own personal login details. Once logged in, access your course and locate the required activity.

For more information and help on how to use kerboodle! visit **www.kerboodle.com**.

How to use this book

Objectives

Look for the list of **Learning Objectives** based on the requirements of this course so you can ensure you are covering everything you need to know for the exam.

AQA Examiner's tip

Don't forget to read the **AQA Examiner's Tips** throughout the book as well as practice answering **Examination-style Questions**.

Visit **www.nelsonthornes.com/aqagcse** for more information.

AQA examination-style questions are reproduced by permission of the Assessment and Qualifications Alliance.

AQA GCSE D&T: Textiles Technology

■ What is Textiles Technology?

Students who opt to study Textiles Technology at GCSE level are keen to design and make creative and unique pieces of textile work. Textiles Technology is a very exciting subject that encourages students to consider technological advances in textiles as well as building up traditional textiles skills, knowledge and understanding. The subject involves:

- Learning about fibres, fabrics and components.
- Being creative and understanding how designers get inspiration for design ideas.
- Understanding the issues that influence textile design and marketing.
- Investigating methods to colour, decorate, and stitch textile products.
- Testing, developing and evaluating ideas.
- Being aware of how textile products are manufactured.
- Knowing about the use of computers in designing and making.

Many textiles technology lessons involve practical work, to explore exciting new textile techniques. You may work with dyes, fibres, threads, yarns, fabrics and components to add colour, pattern, shape and texture to design ideas. Textile skills are taught to understand how to shape and add 3D features and fastenings to products. Some lessons will focus on learning about textile materials and components, perhaps involving product analysis. You will need to know about how designers operate and how textile products are manufactured in order to develop their own successful products.

The GCSE grade will be awarded as a result of completing two units of work:

Unit 1: Written paper

The written paper is two hours long and is worth 40% of the total marks.

Section A: This asks you to design a textile product. During the preparation period for the exam, a pre-release sheet is given to students to ask them to research the design question context. Approximately 25% of the paper marks are for Section A.

Section B: These questions will be based on the subject content listed in the Specification. It will test your subject knowledge and understanding. Approximately 75% of the paper marks are for Section B.

Unit 2: Design and making practice

You will be required to select a design brief from a list of Controlled Assessment Tasks. A concise design folder and a made piece will be completed in the classroom over a period of approximately 45 hours. Students should include photographs of the finished product as well as photographs at various stages of the making.

The design and making activity is worth 60% of the total marks.

How will this book help?

This book has been written to support you in your preparation for the written paper and to help you respond to the controlled assessment task with confidence. This book should also help you to:

- be aware of technological advances and the use of modern textile materials and components
- understand environmental issues including sustainable designs, waste reduction, recycling of textiles, organic and fairtrade cotton, bio fibres and biodegradable fabrics
- consider the importance and benefits of ICT including CAD/CAM to assist in the production of textile products
- work creatively with a focus on innovative designing.

The book is divided into two units which match the AQA GCSE Textiles Technology Specification:

Unit 1 Written paper

- Materials and components
- Design and market influences
- Processes and manufacture.

Unit 2 Designing and making practice

Each section of the book offers very clear information with helpful Learning Objectives, AQA Examiner's Tips, Remember, Summaries, Key Terms and Links to further information. Informative photographs include exemplar student design folder sheets, to illustrate how other students have worked. Activities are provided to encourage you to enjoy working independently on set tasks. Understanding is encouraged through use of Case Studies which explain how real designers and textile companies operate. At the end of each Unit 1 section, examination-style questions are listed to help you practice answering questions on each section.

Future career opportunities in Textiles Technology

Studying Textiles Technology can lead to a wide variety of exciting and well-paid career opportunities in the fashion, design and textiles industries and education services. For example Textile or Fashion Designer, Trend Forecaster, Fashion Merchandiser, Pattern Maker or Grader, Fashion Stylist, Fashion Editor, Fashion Illustrator, Fashion Photographer, Costume Designer, Personal Stylist and Interior Designer.

This book shows some of these jobs in action in the Case Studies and illustrated in photographs.

Materials and components

Design and technology involves the study of materials and components. To understand textiles technology we have to start with how fabrics are made and what characteristics the fabric can have, so that we make an informed decision when we select a fabric for a product. This unit will enable you to learn about where fibres come from, and how fabrics are made, and discover some of the main characteristics of fibres and the properties of fibres and fabrics.

Using this information you should be able to choose fabrics for a project and be able to evaluate fabric choice in products made by others. Once the fabric is chosen it may need a range of components and enhancements to produce the final product; you will be given information to help you understand these choices. It is also important to understand that textiles technology is an ever-changing industry, and we not only see lots of new products designed each year, but there are also new fibres, fabrics, finishes and components being developed.

■ What will you study in this section?

After completing Materials and components (Chapters 1–3) you should have a good understanding of:

- how to make an informed fabric and component choice for a product
- where fibres come from and the characteristics of fibres when used as fabrics
- the construction of fabrics and how this affects how a fabric performs
- the properties of fabrics; finishes and components
- the industrial approach to fabric choice
- the labelling of fabrics and textile products
- some new technological developments in fibres, fabrics and components
- some ways of changing fabrics through manipulation and enhancement.

■ Making techniques

One of the areas covered in this section is about using fabrics and components in a practical way to achieve effective outcomes. You will learn many product construction and fabric enhancement techniques during your GCSE course; this unit covers some of the techniques you may be testing and selecting when:

- printing and dying fabrics
- stitching and decorating fabrics
- manipulating and folding fabrics.

How will you use the information?

When you have studied this section it is very important to use the knowledge gained in both the controlled assessment and the examination. You will need to investigate possible fabrics and components and select for practical outcomes you will make and for products you may design in an examination. You will be tested on your knowledge of fabrics, components, finishes, techniques and all the effects these selections have on a product. You also need to consider the consumer's point of view, as well as the industrial requirements, and the wider global issues related to fabric and component choice.

kerboodle!

1.1 Choosing fibres and fabrics

What are fibres?

Fibres are fine hair-like structures that are either short (**staple**) or long (**filament**). These fibres are made into **yarns** and **fabrics**.

What is a fabric?

Fabrics are made up of fibres. These fibres have either been twisted into yarns and then knitted or woven together to make a length of the fabric, or they have been formed into a web and heat pressed or glued together as a non-woven fabric.

A fabric can be made up of one or more fibres and could have a special finish applied. There are thousands of fabrics to choose from and new fabrics are being developed all the time.

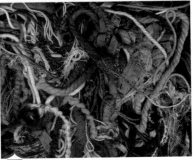

A *Yarns*

How do I choose the best fabric for my design?

There are many factors to consider and questions to answer when choosing a fabric, including the following:

- What must it be able to do when made into the product?
- What would look good for this product?
- How much of a budget have I got to spend on fabric?
- What is fashionable in fabric at the moment?
- What have other designers chosen for similar products?
- Does anyone have any demands on my choice? (Customer/company restraints)
- What choices of fabric are available to me?
- Can I get the fabric in the colour or pattern that I have designed?
- Are there any special properties that I would like my fabric to have?
- Are there any new developments in fabrics that would improve my design?
- Will my fabric choice affect the popularity of my product?
- Will my fabric choice affect the quality and/or the care of my product?
- Will I still be able to make my product if I use this fabric?
- Will I need to buy any special equipment to work with this fabric?

The answers are important; the decisions made can completely change a design for the better – or for the worse if taken too lightly.

B *Fabrics*

Activity

Find four different textile products and discuss the fabric choices made, using the list of factors as your guide. Explain each and suggest alternative equally good or improved choices. Present your findings.

The following case study describes a trade fair (an exhibition put on by fabric manufacturers to sell their new fabrics to customers all over the world). There are stalls set out with fabrics for customers to see and touch, and many exhibitors make up some of their fabrics into garments; some include small fashion shows, to try and show customers how good their fabrics look as fashion items.

AQA *Examiner's tip*

Fabric choice and justification for a fabric is an important skill and is often tested in examinations, as well as in made products.

∞links

Find out more at **www.associatedcontent.com** – search for Sewing 101: How to choose fabric.

The Intertex Milano Trade Fair

Textile trade fairs take place all over the world and the Intertex Milano (which attracts around 25,000 buyers) is just one example.

The fair is open to manufacturers, designers, importers, wholesalers, volume retailers, department stores, chain stores, private label producers and brand names. It takes place over a few days and is a showcase for Italian fabric and accessory manufacturers. The five focus sectors of the fair are:

- Jeans World – for trousers, jackets and T-shirts
- Luxury – for cocktail dresses, evening wear and wedding gowns
- Intimates – for underwear, lingerie and beachwear
- Knitwear – for cashmeres, merino wools and rich blends
- Fashion accessories – for men and women in silk, leather, and silver and semi-precious stones.

Designers are sent by their companies to select possible fabrics for their future collections or just to make contact with up-and-coming textile producers.

www.biztradeshows.com/intertex-milano/

Case study

E *The Intertex Milano Trade fair*

Summary

One of the key factors in choosing an appropriate fabric is what it is made from.

All needs must be considered before making a fabric selection.

A trade show is an opportunity for fabric manufacturers to sell their fabrics to product manufacturers and designers.

What are natural fibres and where do they come from?

A fibre is a thin, hair-like structure that can be short or long. If the fibre is short it is called a staple fibre and if long it is called a filament fibre. Short staple fibres need to be spun into yarns and tend to have a slightly hairy appearance, whereas long filament fibres give a smooth finish to fabrics.

Natural fibres are found in natural surroundings; there are two classifications, with fibres being either animal or plant based. All natural fibres have to be processed to make them suitable for use as yarns and fabrics.

The table below shows where natural fibres come from.

A *Where natural fibres come from*

Plant-based fibre	Where it comes from
Cotton	Cotton comes from the fine hairs on the seeds in a ripe seed pod of a cotton plant
Linen	Linen comes from the fibrous stem of a flax plant
Some other vegetable fibres	Kapok hair cells come from the kapok fruit Hemp fibres come from the hemp plant
Animal-based fibre	**Where it comes from**
Wool	Wool comes from the hair of sheep; this hair is often known as a coat or fleece
Silk	Silk is a fibre from the cocoon of a silkworm. The outer layer tends to be short staple (broken cocoon) and the inner layer comprises long filament fibres carefully unravelled
Some other animal hairs used to make yarns	Cashmere comes from a goat's fine undercoat Camel hair is collected from camels, not shorn Mohair is from the angora goat Angora hair is from the angora rabbit

What are the main properties of natural fibres and fabrics?

Fibres are all unique, with their own set of characteristics, advantages and disadvantages. These are called properties. Sometimes one fibre is mixed or blended with another to improve its properties; you will learn much more about this on pages 22–23.

The following table will help you learn about those properties and also inform you when selecting fabrics for products.

links

Find out more at
www.wildfibres.co.uk

B *Flax plant*

C *Silk cocoons*

D *Angora rabbit*

E *The properties and characteristics of fibres*

Properties	Cotton	Linen	Silk	Wool
Physical	Strong, absorbent, cool to wear, hard-wearing, creases easily	Very hard-wearing, cool next to skin, strong, absorbent and creases easily, has no drape	Absorbent, soft and comfortable, cool and warm	Warm, absorbent, low flammability
Aesthetic	Smooth, versatile, easy to care for and enhance	Has a natural look and dull lustre, good **handle**	Natural sheen, handles well and strong when dry	Good handle, elasticity
Characteristics in use				
Fabric names	Calico Corduroy Denim Drill Poplin Velvet	Duck Huckabuck	Chiffon Crêpe Dupion Duchess Organza Taffeta	Lambs Merino Superwash Felt Harris tweed Gaberdine
Uses	Soft furnishings All clothing items Yarns for knitting	Lightweight clothing often for summer wear Soft furnishings, tea towels and table linen	Luxury clothing Soft furnishings Knitwear	Warm outer wear Lightweight wool for suiting and knitwear Soft furnishings, carpets, blankets
Advantages	Strong when wet Durable Reasonably inexpensive Environmentally sustainable Comfortable to wear	Stronger when wet Smooth finish Very hard-wearing Highly absorbent Comfortable fabric to wear	Soft, smooth sheen, lustrous finish Drapes well Comfortable to wear next to the skin	Warm, can be produced in a wide range of weights of fabrics Comfortable, does not crease easily
Disadvantages	Creases easily Burns easily Shrinks	Creases badly Can be expensive	Expensive Can be weaker when wet and may not wash well May crease easily	May shrink when washed Absorbent so takes a long time to dry May (for some types) feel uncomfortable and itchy next to skin

Remember

Natural fibres come from sustainable sources.

Activity

Using basic textile products, such as clothing, soft furnishings and bags, check the labels and collect together all those with 100 per cent natural fibres in all or part of the product. Write an evaluation of the properties and give reasons why you think the designer has selected the natural fibre for this product. Can you suggest an alternative natural fibre?

Summary

Natural fibres are very versatile and widely used in textile products.

There are two types of fibre: staple and filament.

There are two main natural sources of fibres: plant and animal.

Natural fibres have a wide range of properties that need to be considered when selecting fabrics for textile products.

What are synthetic fibres and where do they come from?

Synthetic fibres are artificial fibres; they are made from synthetic polymers, which come from oil, coal and other petrol-based chemicals (monomers). The process of joining these monomers is known as **polymerisation**, and then the mixed polymers are spun (twisted) into yarns.

Synthetic fibres fall into groups based on the polymer that the fibres are made from, such as the three that are most commonly used in textiles: acrylic, polyamide (Nylon), polyester. There are others you may be aware of such as elastane (Lycra), polyvinyl chloride (PVC) and polypropylene (used in carpets). Synthetic fibres, which are made in chemical plants by a range of companies across the world, are given **trade names**. For example, the elastane fibre produced by DuPont has the trade name Lycra and the polyamide invented by DuPont in 1938 is named Nylon.

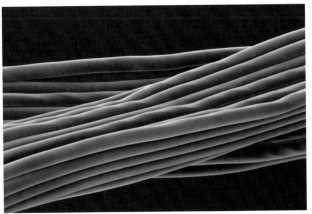

A *Microscopic view of three synthetic fibres: polyamide, Lycra and polyester*

Developments in synthetic fibres and fabrics

Companies such as DuPont continue to research and develop new synthetic fibres:

Key terms

Synthetic fibre: entirely artificial and made using oil and coal in its chemical production.

Polymerisation: the process by which monomers are joined together to form polymers.

Trade name: a name given to a fibre created and sold by a company such as Nylon (named by DuPont) – where polyamide is its generic name.

Microfibre: a synthetic fibre that is made 60 times finer than a human hair.

- **Microfibres** are thin, hair-like fibres made from polyamide or polyester. These fibres can be made up to 60 times thinner than a human hair, which makes them lightweight; they are strong and water repellent but also absorbent, breathable and have a very good 'handle' or feel. The most common products made from microfibres are underwear, sportswear, hosiery and water-repellent outdoor wear, but designers are using these fibres more and more in their fashion collections. Tactel Micro is often seen today as a label on sportswear or underwear; Meryl Micro is used in active sportswear.

- Tactel Aquator was designed by DuPont for its moisture-management properties. It is a non-absorbent fibre that takes moisture away from the body.

- Hi-tech, very strong fibres such as Kevlar and Cordura were developed for industrial use, but they are now being used for active outerwear for many extreme sports and activities that require a high degree of resistance to abrasion.

links

Find out more at
www.dupont.com

B *Microfibre*

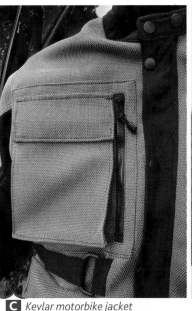
C *Kevlar motorbike jacket*

D *Perma-pleat*

What are the main properties of synthetic fibres and fabrics?

Synthetic fibres can be developed to have many different appearances and properties. They can be made as filament or staple fibres; they can be bulked or crimped to give more volume; they can be made up as microfibres; and they can encapsulate chemicals, perhaps to give anti-bacterial properties or to be perfume scented.

Because synthetic fibres are plastics based, they have thermosetting and thermoplastic properties. These allow the fibres to be manipulated using heat, to create permanent pleats in fabrics and add textures, for example.

The following table lists some of the properties of synthetic fibres.

E *Properties of synthetic fibres*

Characteristics in use	Polyamide	Polyester	Acrylic	Elastane
Physical	Strong, hard-wearing, good elasticity, thermoplastic, does not decompose, melts as it burns Resists most alkalis, but can be damaged by strong acids	Very strong when wet and dry, flame resistant, thermoplastic, does not decompose Resists most alkalis unless very concentrated, but is damaged by strong acids	Strong but weaker when wet, thermoplastic, shrinks from heat and burns slowly, then melts	Very elastic, lightweight but still very strong, resists chemicals and biological damage from perspiration Very hard-wearing
Aesthetic	Versatile, can be made into many finishes	Versatile, can be made into many finishes	Soft, can be made into fine and coarse staple fibres	Medium to coarse filament fibres
Fabric names	Nylon Tactel Tactel Micro	Terylene Polyester fleece Trevira Finesse Miratec Dacron	Courtelle Amicor	Lycra
End use	Clothing Ropes Carpets and rugs Seat-belts and sports belting	Wide range of textile products	Knitwear and knitted jersey fabrics Toys, fake-fur products Upholstery fabrics Anti-bacterial socks and sportswear	Swimwear, sportswear and all clothing that may require extra elasticity, such as easy-fit jeans or fitted blouses (Elastane fibres are always combined with a higher percentage of another fibre in these products, e.g. stretch jeans are 96% cotton/4% elastane)
Advantages	Strong when wet Durable Reasonably inexpensive Resists bacteria	Strong when wet, dries quickly Cheap Hard-wearing Resists bacteria	Can be made warm, insulating and soft	Very stretchy, keeps its shape, can resist sun and sea, lightweight but strong
Disadvantages	Poor absorbency Can be damaged by sunlight, making it discolour and become weaker	Very poor absorbency	Poor absorbency	Very poor absorbency

F *Polyamide/Lycra swimming wear*   **G** *Acrylic school jumper*

Activities

1 Using the table, name and describe a polyamide synthetic fibre.

2 Why do you think synthetic fibres are poor absorbers of liquids?

3 Name a suitable synthetic fibre or combination of synthetic fibres for the following products:

   ■ a swimsuit

   ■ a pair of tights

   ■ a football shirt

   ■ a car seat belt

   ■ a child's toy.

Explain your choices for each product.

4 Elastane is becoming more commonly used in clothing by designers: name four textile products that could be made from this fibre and explain the advantages of using elastane for each product you choose.

5 What is a microfibre?

◯◯ links

Find out more at
www.lycra.com

Remember

Lycra is a rubber-based fibre; it is never used on its own in a product but is added in small percentages to give extra stretch and better fit.

AQA Examiner's tip

You need to be able to name some synthetic fibres and give reasons why a synthetic fabric has been chosen for a particular product. The main reasons for the choice will become clear if you think about the properties of these fibres.

Summary

Synthetic fibres are artificial and use up natural resources such as coal and oil.

Synthetic fibres can be made to have many properties and are very versatile.

Synthetic fibres are poor absorbers of liquids owing to their polymer origins (polymer is very like a plastic).

1.4 Regenerated fibres and fabrics

What are regenerated fibres and where do they come from?

Regenerated fibres are similar to cotton, they were the first of the manufactured fibres to be developed. They are made from cellulose-based fibres that originate from plants such as wood pulp; a chemical is added to extract the cellulose fibres. The classification of the fibre relates to the chemical solvent system used to extract the fibre, so regenerated fibres are part natural and part artificial.

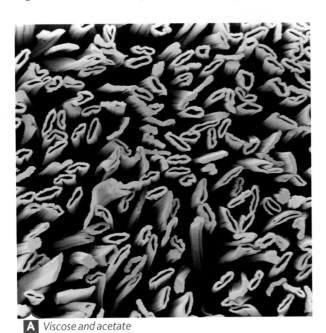 

A *Viscose and acetate*

Types of regenerated fibres

- Regenerated fibres can be filament or staple; they can be given many textures and properties like synthetic fibres.
- The most recent developments in regenerated fibres have made them more environmentally friendly by making the production of the fibre low energy (low in the use of fossil fuels) and by using the **closed-loop process** (waste created in manufacture is reused in the production process).
- Viscose, rayon, acetate, triacetate, modal, Tencel and Lyocell are all regenerated fibres.
- Viscose can be used as a filament yarn, woven or knitted into lustrous fabrics and crêpe fabrics, but as a staple fibre can blend with other fibres to add lustre and absorbency.
- Acetate and triacetate are often known as a cheap silk alternative owing to their elegant drape and lustre.
- Tencel and Lyocell are made so they are fully recyclable and **biodegradeable**; high strength when wet, minimal shrinkage and

good dye absorbancy make them a popular blended fibre. Owing to its high wet strength and absorbancy, Lyocell can also be used as a non-woven fabric for wipes and swabs in medical situations and even for disposable gowns for medical staff.

⊕links

Find out more at
www.tencel.com
www.fibersource.com

B *Regenerated fibres*

Properties of regenerated fibres

As regenerated fibres are from a plant-based source, their properties are similar to those of cotton. They are:

- highly absorbent
- washable
- soft
- smooth
- comfortable to wear
- and have good drape.

Uses of regenerated fibres

Owing to their properties, regenerated fibres are widely used in clothing; they can be given different finishes to make them smooth, shiny or textured. Common uses are fashion clothing, lingerie and trimmings such as ribbons. With new developments, regenerated fibres are becoming more technically advanced and are used in protective clothing and breathable fabrics and in items for medical use.

The development of Lyocell

Lyocell is a fabric made from a tree; it is soft, flowing, cool and comfortable and needs little ironing. It has silk-like properties when it comes to feel and look but has cotton-like properties when it comes to strength and care. Where did this miracle fabric come from?

So who invented it?

The original process was invented by Akzo Nobel and then licensed to Courtaulds in the 1970s, Courtaulds developed the first stable process to produce Lyocell fibre in the late 1980s and the brand name was **Tencel**. Courtaulds discovered, over time (in the 1990s), that Lyocell has great capacity for dye yields, with more vibrant colours being produced than in cotton or viscose while using less dye; colourfastness was also good.

What is it made of and how is it made?

The raw material is cellulose, which tends to be from recycled paper which has a solvent added which is called amine oxide. The cellulose is then passed through holes in a steel plate (spinnerets); their precise design and manufacture is critical to the successful formation of the filaments. The production system is called closed–loop; it is short and compact, allowing low costs, no waste and low energy use, making this fibre an environmentally friendly one. It also means the fibre is biodegradable, recyclable and from **sustainable** sources.

What are its other advantages apart from the environmental ones?

It is very strong when wet, even stronger than cotton. It doesn't stretch or shrink when wet or dry unlike cotton and viscose.

It feels soft, drapes well and can be blended with both natural and synthetic fibres.

Are there any disadvantages?

It can be expensive to dye owing to the types of dyes required to colour it and it does fibrillate, which causes pilling (where small balls of the fibre form on the surface), but developments with Tencel have been successful in producing a non-fibrillating version that has a great capacity for dye yields.

What about its future?

Lyocell is constantly being developed; it can have various finishes applied: one of the most popular is the 'peach skin' appearance and feel. New developments in the denim industry make this fibre suitable for the dark denim trend, giving the fabric a much softer, more comfortable feel. Although Tencel can be a little more expensive, its great range of properties have moved it into the non-woven market for medical supplies, filtration media (tea bags), feminine hygiene products, and sewing threads. The future of this fibre is bright: it could replace some viscose and polyester production and even be a substitute for cotton as the process is more compact and not prey to weather conditions as cotton is.

Key terms

Sustainable: can be manufactured with little or no negative impact on the environment and on the health and wellbeing of the workers employed to make the product.

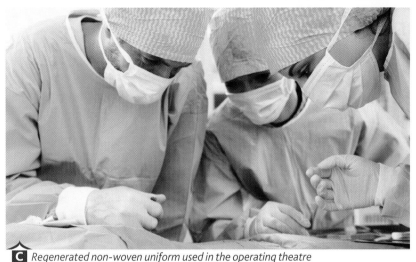

C *Regenerated non-woven uniform used in the operating theatre*

D *Tencel label and clothing*

Summary

Regenerated fibres are a combination of natural and artificial.

Regenerated fibres can be made to have many properties and are very versatile.

Regenerated fibres are similar to cotton and are therefore good absorbers.

AQA Examiner's tip

Questions are often related to environmentally friendly fabrics or processes; the regenerated fibres produced in a closed-loop process is a good example to use.

1.5 Blended and mixed fibres

What is a blended fibre?

A **blended fibre** is a combination of two or more fibres spun together when the yarn is made. The most common example of this is the cotton polyester blend. Cotton is a cool, soft, strong, comfortable fabric and polyester is hard-wearing, lightweight, a poor absorber and elastic; combining them in one fabric gives the comfort and cool feel of cotton but with the hard-wearing, quick-drying and crease-resisting properties of polyester. It is easy to see why this is a popular blend.

A *Polycotton school shirt*

B *Tight-fitting denim jeans*

Many other combinations are also desirable. For example, blending wool with nylon will make it more hard-wearing and it will be an easier fabric to care for. For these reasons this combination is often used in carpeting. Silk is a very expensive fibre, but, blended with polyester or one of the regenerated fibres, it becomes much cheaper to produce and can be easier to wash.

Many of the regenerated fibres are blended with synthetic fibres as they can be manufactured to an exact specification for a particular purpose, for use in many industrial products.

What is a mixed fibre?

A **mixed fibre** is where one type of yarn is mixed with at least one other in the fabric production.

A common example is the mix of cotton yarns with Lycra yarns to give extra stretch and comfort to denim jeans, fitted shirts and swimwear. Mixes can also be made for **aesthetic** reasons such as in two-tone fabrics: for example, silk taffeta using black and red yarns to give the desired effect, or denim jeans with blue and white yarns.

The main reasons for blended and mixed fibres

Blended fibres and mixed yarn fabrics are produced for the following reasons:

- to improve the appearance of a fabric (i.e. texture, colour and tone)
- to improve the quality of the fabric so that it is more durable, stronger and can be more easily cared for
- to improve the handle of a fabric so that it drapes better, is easier to sew and can keep its shape well
- to improve the profitability of a fabric so that is cheaper to produce, and more desirable to customers.

New blends and mixes of fibres and fabrics

Manufacturers have been developing new fibres and fabrics since the first animal skin was used, and research and development continues each year. Different combinations give a wide range of fabrics for designers and consumers to choose from and improvements in this area are always being made. New **green fibres** from plants and other natural sustainable sources, such as leaves and vegetables, are constantly being tested.

Peat has been used in Scandinavia to make fibres that are rather like wool and felt; a company called Kultaturve has developed and designed a range of clothing for these fibres.

Most of these green fibres can be blended and mixed with other fibres to improve their qualities; the peat fibre is often blended with other natural fibres to enhance its natural characteristics.

links

Find out more at
www.ecotopia.be/yearbook/
fashion.html

AQA   Examiner's tip

You need to be able to justify why blends of fibres are produced and why mixes of yarns are made into fabrics. It is always good to be able to give examples.

Activities

1   What is the difference between a blended and a mixed fabric?

2   Give three reasons for blending or mixing a fibre.

3   Using books and the internet find out what unusual plant sources have been used to make green fibres.

Summary

Blended and mixed fibres provide a wide range of fibres and fabrics for designers, manufacturers and customers.

Fibres can be blended and mixed in many combinations to enhance fabric properties.

New blends and mixes of fibres and yarns are being developed each year by textile research and development teams.

Woven fabrics

Weaving is one of the most common ways of making a two-dimensional **woven fabric**. The yarns are interlaced at right angles to each other during the process of weaving: the yarn that is horizontal is called the **weft** yarn; and the yarn that goes vertically is known as the **warp** yarn. As it runs vertically down the length of the fabric, the warp yarn is also referred to as the **grain** line. If you put a ruler or tape measure diagonally across the fabric, you are finding the **bias**. At the edge of a woven piece of fabric the weft yarns wrap around the warp yarns and this is called the **selvedge**.

The weaving is done on a loom: if the weave is simple it will be done on a shuttle loom, but if the weave is complicated with complex weaves then it will be done on a **Jacquard** loom.

Types of weaves

Plain weave

Plain weave is the simplest and tightest weave. The weft yarn goes over and under alternate warp yarns; the closer the yarns the denser the fabric. This fabric looks the same on both sides and is the cheapest to make. Examples of plain weave fabrics are calico, taffeta, Habutai silk, voile, cotton shirting and muslin.

Twill weave

Twill weave is slightly more complicated. The weft yarn goes over more than one warp yarn and is recognisable by a diagonal stripe on the fabric. This is a strong weave for soft yarns, such as wools and cottons used to make tartan, tweed, denim and gabardine.

Satin or sateen weaves

Satin weaves (or sateen weaves) are created in a uniform way in which either the warp or the weft floats over four or more yarns to give a real sheen to the fabric. Examples are duchess satin, crêpe-backed satin and silk charmeuse.

Other weaves

Plain, twill and satin weaves can be combined in many ways to produce ribs and other types of patterns. Jacquard weaves have complex patterns such as flowers, leaves and lettering. You often see these weaves on white tablecloths, evening wear and soft furnishings such as curtains. **Pile weaves** are woven with an extra layer of weft yarns that form loops on the surface of the fabric; these can be left as loops or cut. Velvet and corduroy are examples of cut-pile weaves and terry towelling is a looped pile.

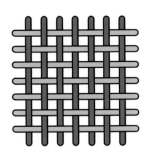

A Plain weave

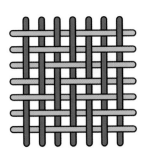

B Twill weave

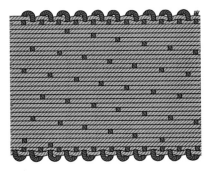

C Satin weave

Properties of woven fabrics

Woven fabrics have the following properties:

- Edges do not fray until cut, as they have a selvedge.
- Once the fabric is cut it will fray.
- They can be woven at different densities and have different **weights**.
- The fabric is at its strongest on the grain line.
- The fabric can stretch on the bias (diagonal) of the fabric.

D *Examples of woven products*

links

Visit **www.fabrics.net/weaves.asp**

Key terms

Woven fabric: interlacing yarns with warp running down the length and weft running across the fabric.

Jacquard: a complex weave or a loom for complex weaves.

Plain weave: a simple basic weave with alternating yarns between weft and warp.

Twill weave: weft goes under more than one warp thread, making a diagonal stripe pattern on the fabric.

Satin weave: the weft or the warp goes over four or more yarns, giving a high, smooth sheen to the fabric.

Pile weave: loops or cut loops form a raised texture on the fabric.

Weight: of a fabric is dictated by the thickness and fibre type of the yarn and/or the denseness of the weave or knit.

AQA *Examiner's tip*

Make sure you recognise and can label a woven fabric. Remember, weft is left to right and warp is up and down!

Activities

1. Make a collection of woven fabric samples and label each by type of weave. Look under a magnifying glass if you are not sure; fraying the edges will help your investigation.

2. Design a new tartan check using colour and weaving combinations. Your tartan should reflect fashion trends and teenage culture. (You may wish to use graph paper for this task.)

Summary

Weaving is one of the most common ways of making a fabric.

A woven fabric has weft yarns and warp yarns.

A selvedge is on the two edges of the fabric, parallel to the grain line.

The grain line follows the warp yarns.

The bias is diagonally across the grain, where the fabric will stretch.

Non-woven fabrics

Non-woven fabrics are made in two main ways: they are either **felted** or they are **bonded**. The fabrics use fibres rather than yarns; these are laid randomly or in a uniform way to make weblike layers. They are held together by either the felting or bonding process.

Felted fabrics

Wool felt is the most common non-woven fabric and is produced by using short staple fibres from wool or other animal hairs (such as camel). Wool is an ideal fibre because its surface has natural hook-like scales, which, when moisture, heat and vigorous movement are applied, interlock with each other. The heat and damp conditions cause the fibres to curl up, and the scales locking together prevents the fibres from straightening out again. When you wash a natural wool jumper and it shrinks in size the jumper is actually felting, and you can't make it bigger again no matter how hard you try to stretch it back.

Bonded fabrics

There are three main methods of making bonded fabrics:

- **Dry laid** – a web of fibres is laid in a drum and hot air is injected to bond the fibres together.
- **Wet laid** – a web of fibres is mixed with a solvent that softens the fibres and releases a glue-like substance that bonds the fibres together and then the web is laid out to dry.
- **Direct spun** – the fibres are spun on to a conveyer belt and glues are sprayed on to the fibres, which are then pressed to bond; if the fibres are thermoplastic (will change shape with heat) then the glue is not needed in this process.

What are felted and bonded fabrics used for?

Hats, jackets, coats, toys and snooker table covers are some common uses for wool felts.

Bonded fabrics are used for disposable products such as cloths, medical masks and table linen. They are also used for interfacings for stiffening and strengthening clothing and in dressmaking (e.g. Vilene).

Objectives

Learn what a non-woven fabric is.

Learn how it is made.

Learn about its properties.

A *A snooker table cover is made from wool felt*

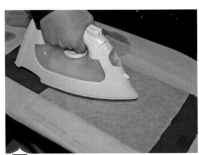

B *Using interfacing on a product*

What are the properties of these non-woven fabrics?

Non-woven fabrics:

- are not very strong
- can be made in a range of weights
- do not fray
- can be made into moulded shapes
- can be made from recycled fibres
- can be made to be soluble
- can be made to soften with heat and act like a glue (used for hemming)
- can easily pill (bobbles from on the surface)
- may be weaker when wet
- can be made permeable (water can pass through)
- are cheap to produce
- will also take on some of the properties of the fibre used in the web (e.g. wool felt is warm and insulating; polyester wadding is lightweight and elastic).

Laminated fabrics

Laminated fabrics are made by bonding two or more fabrics together. Many fabrics require extra insulation or protection, and foam is bonded to provide this. Sometimes comfort can be an issue with **PVC** fabrics, so a softer fabric may be bonded instead of using a lining. Making a fabric breathable and waterproof may require lamination of a membrane, as in Gortex and Sympatex.

New technology in non-woven fabrics

Non-woven fabric production such as felting and bonding is often used by manufacturers when producing fabrics with some of the new vegetable-based yarns, as these tend to have shorter staple fibres. Designers are able to design their own original fabrics with the felting method. The industrial application of non-woven fabrics is ever-increasing and includes filtration systems, medical uses and insulating purposes. The development of **micro-encapsulation** technology (enabling active substances to be fixed to the surface of the fibre or fabric) means many non-woven fabrics can be perfumed or anti-bacterial. Newer fibres like Lyocell can be made into non-woven fabrics, giving better absorption and high wet strength for products such as medical swabs.

Summary

Non-woven fabrics are felted or bonded together.

Non-woven fabrics have many uses in textile products, particularly as internal strengtheners and to assist sewing, such as interfacing.

Many non-woven fabrics are disposable products.

Laminated fabrics may not be non-woven but bonded together with heat or glue.

links

Find out more at
www.gorefabrics.com
www.sympatex.com

Key terms

Felted: fibres are pressed together using heat, moisture and agitation, or hot needles.

Bonded: webs of fibres are pressed together using adhesives or heat.

Laminated: two or more fabrics bonded together to enhance the fabric's properties.

PVC: polyvinyl chloride.

Micro-encapsulation: substances that are fixed to the fabric or the fibre and can then be activated, such as perfumes.

Activities

1 Using a sample of felt, examine it, look at it through a magnifier, try to pull it apart and record your findings.

2 In your classroom consider how many products have or could have been made using non-woven fabrics; explain how and why you think these fabrics were chosen for each product. (You will be wearing some!)

AQA Examiner's tip

You must be able to identify the appropriate use of non-woven fabrics, especially when the fabric is used as a component in a product, to improve quality.

Knitted fabrics

A knitted fabric is made of interlocking loops, using one or more yarns. If the loops are broken the fabric will come apart easily. There are two types of knitted fabric: **weft knit** and **warp knit**.

Weft-knitted fabrics

- A single yarn can be used. Knitting can be done by hand or machine.
- The fabric is made by forming interlocking loops of yarn across the width or on a round.
- This type of knit can unravel and form a ladder.

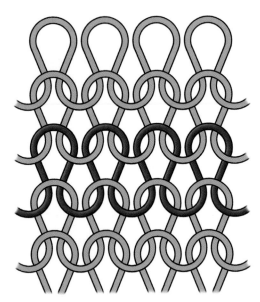

A Weft knit

Characteristics of weft knit

- Fabric has high elasticity and stretch.
- Loops trap air and retain heat.
- There are two sides to the fabric and they are easily identifiable.
- Fabric can lose shape easily.
- Fabric unravels and ladders when pulled and cut.

Type of weft-knit fabric

Single jersey: this is used for T-shirts, sweaters, ribbed socks and jumpers, sportswear and fake fur. An example is a 100 per cent wool polo-neck weft-knit jumper.

Warp-knitted fabrics

- The yarn loops in a vertical direction; the fabric is held together by interlocking vertical loops on alternate sides.
- The fabric does not become unravelled and therefore will not form a ladder.

Characteristics of warp knit

- The production system is fast.
- Fabric is elastic but can keep its shape.
- Fabric is hard to unravel, less likely to ladder so can be cut and sewn more easily than weft knit.
- The machine is complicated and therefore more expensive to produce.

Type of warp-knit fabrics

Lock knit: this is used for bed sheets, furnishing fabrics, velour, swimwear fabrics, lace and nets, and fleece fabrics. An example is a pair of 97 per cent polyamide, 3 per cent Lycra warp-knit tights.

New technology in knitted fabrics

The use of computer aided design (CAD) and computer aided manufacture (CAM) technology has allowed designs to become more complex and for visual trials to be made on a computer screen. A knitter can make changes via a keyboard and has the opportunity to be innovative in the styles produced. Owing to advances in knitting technology, items such as heart valves can be produced and garments that have no seams (e.g. underwear) are becoming more commonplace.

links

Find out more at
www.industrial-fabrics.co.uk

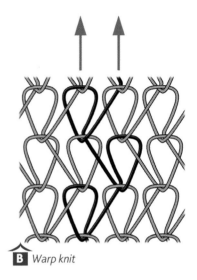

B *Warp knit*

AQA Examiner's tip

Make sure you can recognise and label a knitted fabric. Remember, weft is left to right (think hand knitting) and warp is up and down!

Activities

1. Name three products that can be made by knitted construction. Explain what this method could add to the products.

2. Name two disadvantages of a knitted fabric.

3. Name three advantages of a knitted fabric.

4. Why are some weft-knitted items done by hand, not machine?

5. How can information and communication technology (ICT) help with the design and development of new knitted products?

6. Find some samples of knitted fabrics; identify the type of knit and name a product they could be made into.

Summary

Knitted fabrics are made by warp and weft knitting.

Knitted fabrics can be designed in a virtual programme on the computer.

CAM equipment can speed up the manufacturing process.

The main qualities of knitwear are stretch, comfort and warmth.

Most garments can be made from knitted fabrics.

1.9 Fabric finishes

What is a fabric finish?

Once a fabric has been produced it often goes through a finishing process to improve its appearance and/or properties. The main types of finishes are as follows:

- physical – where a machine or tool is used to change the fabric
- chemical – where chemicals are used to change the fabric
- biological – where bacteria and enzymes are used on cellulose-based (plant-based) fibres
- coated – where the fabric is coated on one side with a substance (such as Teflon, to repel staining).

Why are fabric finishes used?

Finishes have been developed to improve the fabric in many ways such as:

- enhance appearance – colour, pattern, sheen
- change texture – **embossing**, brushing, smoothing
- improve feel – softer, crisper, firmer
- improve **drape** – weighted
- modify wearing qualities – crease resistance, stain resistance, flammability, waterproof, etc.
- modify care requirements – easy wash, quicker drying times, **colourfast**, less shrinkage.

A *Embossed fabric*

Key terms

Embossing: a relief print pressed into a fabric changing its surface texture as well as giving a patterned appearance.

Drape: how a fabric hangs.

Colourfast: how well a fabric keeps dyes applied to it, even through regular washing.

Finish processes and properties

The following table gives some common fabric finishes and their properties as a guide to fabric choice.

links

Find out more at
www.indiafashionexpo.com

B *Common fabric finishes and their properties*

Type of finish	Description of finish	Change made to fabric
Mechanical		
Brushing	Wire rollers brush the surface of the fabric	Fabric has a napped (raised) surface and handle is softer
Embossing	Engraved rollers create a relief pattern on the fabric	Texture and appearance change due to pattern embossed
Calendering	Heavy rollers press the surface of the fabric	Fabric is smoother and has improved sheen
Pressing	Presses smooth the surface of the fabric	There is improved handle and a smoother surface; pressing is often used on wool fabrics
Shrinkage	Fabric is steamed and placed over a vibrating conveyer belt	This reduces further shrinkage later (in use and care)
Chemical		
Water-repellent	Silicone is sprayed on to the fabric surface	Droplets of water remain on the surface; air can pass through. This is not waterproofing and fabric will let water through if saturated
Stain-resistant	Stain-resistant resins are applied to the surface of the fabric	Dirt is prevented from clinging to the surface
Crease-resistant	Resins are applied to fabric	Fabrics are crisper but crease less
Flame-resistant	Chemicals are applied to yarn or fabric	This prevents fabric from easily igniting
Shrink-resistant	Fibre scales (found on wool) are removed with chlorine, or resins block scales	Shrinkage in washing is reduced; used in wool products

Activity

Do a research investigation into five products with finishes. Consider the improvements to the product due to the finish applied in terms of aesthetics, maintenance, feel and improved performance in use and cost. Write down your findings as a report.

AQA Examiner's tip

When you are tested on finishes applied to fabrics you need to be able to suggest one that fits the end use of a product.

Summary

Properties and characteristics of finishes applied to fabrics can affect fabric choice.

Finishes are applied to enhance the performance of a fabric.

What is a smart fabric?

A fabric that can respond to outside influences without human intervention is considered a **smart fabric**:

- A smart fabric can sense certain conditions.
- A smart fabric can react to certain conditions.
- A smart fabric can adapt to certain conditions.

What conditions will activate a smart fabric?

Heat

Thermochromic colour encapsulated into the surface of fabrics or printed on the surface will react to heat and change colour.

An Italian manufacturer has invented fibres that react to heat by becoming tighter when hot, allowing more air to pass through; the fibres expand in the cold, reducing the air flow, to help the wearer acclimatise to the weather conditions.

Moisture

Solvation chromism has been developed mainly for disposable non-woven textiles where a fabric changes colour when wet, for example babies' nappies.

Light

Photochromic fabrics are dyed to respond to light conditions and change colour. These are particularly good for military use, to reduce the need for camouflage net or change of uniform.

Other conditions

A fabric can be activated by power (see below) or time, and in the future there could be many more developments in these areas.

What is an interactive fabric?

An **interactive fabric** incorporates electronics that are reactivated by a power source. These are still smart fabrics – they just require power.

One important fabric development is in conductivity, where the fabric is electrically conductive while being soft and comfortable. This conductivity can be added with metallic fibres, conductive printing inks and metallic coatings on the fabric surface. **Gorix** is a carbonised fibre with conductivity, used in heated car seats and for motorbike clothing. Philips has developed **Soft switch,** which has conductive threads, woven or knitted structures incorporating pressure sensors that can be used as audio devices. Developments making use of solar energy are popular for power sources.

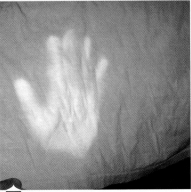

A *Thermochromic dyes used on a T-shirt*

Key terms

Smart fabric: a textile product that changes owing to its environment, without human intervention.

Interactive fabric: a product that requires a power source to activate its features.

AQA Examiner's tip

You need to be aware of technological advancements in fibres, fabrics and products. The ability to name and describe some smart and interactive fabrics is important.

⚭links

Find out more at
www.gorix.com

www.softswitch.co.uk
See Textile components, pages 50–51.

Examples of interactive fabrics include:

- a waistcoat that has conductive fibres so disabled children can communicate
- the life shirt, which monitors blood pressure
- tagging technology, which can track a garment
- paramedics' headwear that can film the patient and be sent to doctors in the hospital
- garments with built-in mobile phone technology
- a tracksuit that can monitor your performance
- gloves with lights to allow cyclists to be seen at night
- heated gloves.

Other developments

Ways of mimicking nature have been widely researched in textile technology. Some examples include the popular **Fastskin** developed by swimwear manufacturer Speedo to be like the surface of a shark's skin, so it channels water away from the body making the swimmer more aerodynamic.

Biomimetics means imitating a living bio system. This process has been used in textile technology by mimicking the natural way a leaf breathes and regulates temperature. **Stomatex** fabric keeps the wearer dry and comfortable during exercise.

Micro-encapsulation has been developed in textiles to allow fibres and fabrics to be impregnated with microscopic bubbles of perfumes, anti-bacterial properties, anti-allergic properties, mosquito repellents and carbon digesters to absorb unpleasant fumes.

Buoyancy and inflatable textiles have been developed such as therma-float for use in buoyancy aids and life jackets, and inflatable yarns in swimwear for children and blow-up bras.

Reflective textiles are used for enhanced safety in cycling and for pedestrians out walking at night, and for sportswear.

Phosphorescent textiles are used for glow-in-the-dark fashions.

Fibre optics are used in trainers for illuminated logos, and fibre-optic sensors are inserted in military garments to detect harmful chemicals.

Nanotechnology in textiles is in its very early stages and is being developed to improve performance of fabrics through controlling particles in fibres and fabrics. Nano-tex is one of the first manufacturers to help clothing firms such Levi and Gap to develop stain-resistant, more durable fabrics.

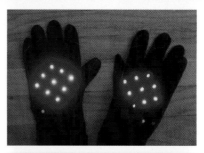

B *Electronics in textiles*

⬭⬭ links

Find out more at
www.nanotextiles.net

Activity

Design a jacket and incorporate into it smart and interactive technology. Present your design as a futuristic product that is fashionable but also addresses some of today's needs. Label it well and say why your design improves on existing designs.

C *Olympic Fastskin swimsuit*

Summary

Smart fabrics react to conditions around them and have many different properties.

Interactive textiles, which use a power source to activate their properties, are becoming more widely used.

Some developments meet a real need and some are more of a novelty design feature.

New textiles are being developed all the time; the possibilities are endless.

2.1 Fabric choice and specification

What is the designer's role in fabric choice?

The role of a product designer within a company is to design products that will sell and make a profit, but their role in choosing the fabric can vary from company to company.

Some companies will give their designers a free choice of fabrics, with only very few limitations such as budget and production issues. Other companies, such as swimwear manufacturers, work in a limited field where the fabric must have certain properties or must be made out of certain fibres. Some companies are identified by their use of the same types of fabrics each year, only changing colours or the weights of the fabrics slightly. Some designers are working in 'green' companies and must restrict their choice to natural, sustainable or **fair trade** types of fabrics.

Designers who do have an input into fabric choice often travel the globe going to fabric trade fairs to see what is available each season. They will also go to fashion shows to see what other designers are using or research the internet to find out what is being developed.

Fabric names and properties

The following table gives some common fabrics and their properties as a guide to fabric choice.

Objectives

Understand the designer's role in fabric choice.

Understand fabric properties, and how they affect choices for products.

Learn about the role of the fabric specification.

Recognise some common fabric names and understand what the properties of these fabrics are.

⚭ links

See Environmental issues and sustainability, pages 82–83.

Key terms

Fair trade: a partnership between producers and consumers that ensures the workers receive a fair wage, better access to markets in developed countries and community support.

A *Some common fabrics and their properties*

Fabric name	Fibre content	Key properties	Suitable products
Denim	100% cotton 94% cotton/6% Lycra	Twill weave, strong, hard-wearing, may shrink, can be made in different weights and can have many finishes applied to change the appearance and feel	Workwear, jeans, jackets, shirts, skirts and dresses Popular for children's wear and in its lightweight form is often used in bedding and other home furnishings
Satin	100% silk 100% rayon 100% polyester	Satin weave, sheen, good drape, weaker when wet, can get water spots (polyester and rayon), smooth and soft to touch. Difficult to sew owing to risk of puckered seams	Bridal and evening wear Underwear Jacket and coat linings
Arctic/Polar fleece	100% polyester 65% acrylic/35% polyester	Knitted, synthetic, lightweight, warm, stretches, wind-proof, soft, breathable, can shed water (such as Polartec Windbloc)	Jackets, sweat tops, sportswear, toys, cushions and dressinggowns

Corduroy	100% cotton 92% cotton/8% Lycra	Woven with a corded pile on the straight grain. Striped appearance, strong and reasonably hard-wearing, soft velvety pile and can be woven into different weights and different widths of cord (e.g. jumbo cord/needle cord)	Skirts, trousers, jackets, children's clothes (Can also be in knitted form and be made into jumpers and stretchy leisure wear)
Tweed	100% wool 100% silk 100% acrylic	Worsted-style woven fabric using two or more colours in the weave. Strong (although silk tweed tends to be more prone to snags and going out of shape) warm, hard-wearing, good crease resistance and can come in a range of weights	Jackets, coats, skirts, suits, trousers and trimmings
Plain weaves – such as cotton shirting, calico, chambray, lawn and gingham	100% cotton 100% linen 50% cotton/50% polyester	Often lightweight weaves, which are strong, crisp, hard-wearing, cool fabrics. Easy to sew and print on, can be woven in two colours, such as chambray and gingham	Shirts, dresses, linings and other lightweight clothing and soft furnishing needs
Ripstop	100% nylon	Lightweight, wind-resistant, durable, water-repellent, does not breathe	Jackets, outdoor wear and bags
Velvet, velveteen and velour	100% cotton 100% rayon 100% silk 100% polyester (microfibre)	Can be woven or knitted; it has a pile that is short and dense (velveteen), or longer and looser, giving more drape and sheen. It is warm and looks luxurious	Dresses, curtains, jackets, coats and upholstery
Drill	100% cotton 94% cotton 6% Lycra	Twill-weave fabric, strong and durable like denim but lighter in weight	Trousers, jackets, workwear overalls, mattress ticking and linings in shoes
Knitted jersey	100% cotton 100% wool 100% silk 100% acrylic 100% polyester All combinations including a small percentage of Lycra	It is a knitted fabric that gives stretch, warmth, movement and fit to a garment. In wool and silk it can have good drape; it will resist wrinkles and with the addition of Lycra can keep its shape	Tops, trousers, leggings, T-shirts and dresses. Can also be used in bedding and soft furnishings
Felt	100% wool 100% synthetic fibres*	Non-woven fabric, does not fray, can be shaped with heat; warm and insulating. Can pill and is weaker when wet	Hats, jackets, coats, toys and craft products, motifs and interfacings

* often recycled fibres (see Fabric construction – non-woven, pages 26–7)

There are many more fabrics to choose from; this table just gives you an idea of the choices and applications of some fabrics. Many of these fabrics can be made in a wide range of fibres, fibre blends and yarn mixes.

Fabric specification

A **fabric specification** is a detailed list of the requirements for the fabric of a particular product. This is often written by the manufacturer rather than the designer so that the designer understands the limitations when selecting fabrics for the prototype.

The following case study is a fabric specification (in the form of a set of questions for the designer to consider before fabric selection) for a company that produces blinds/coverings for windows. After that example you will find a GCSE student-style fabric specification for a child's party dress.

links

Visit
www.apparelsearch.com/
wholesale_clothing/components/
wholesale_fabric.htm

Case study

Lutron guide to fabric specifications

- Qualify the application
- Commercial or residential?
- Multi-purpose or dedicated function rooms?
- Daytime, night-time or all-hours use?
- What types of activities will occur in the space?
- Will an aesthetic match be important inside or outside the building?
- Latitude of project and orientation of windows?
- Additional issues?
- Prioritise needs.

Based on the application, determine priorities including:

- control glare inside (reduce reflections on computer monitors, TVs, etc.)
- provide visual comfort for occupants
- maintain view through windows
- protect interiors from fading
- reduce build-up of heat inside building
- optimise energy efficiency
- achieve a particular aesthetic (inside or outside)
- reduce environmental impact
- create darkened room
- ensure privacy.

If space is multi-purpose, or multiple priorities are equally important, consider a dual-mount application (two fabric rolls mounted on the same window).

Fabric specification for a child's party dress

Main dress fabric:

- must be a shade of pink
- must have lustre/sheen
- should be machine washable
- should be stain-resistant or watermark-resistant
- should be reasonably cheap to buy
- will be woven to keep its shape
- will be smooth and comfortable to wear
- will hold dye well and not lose colour through washing
- should be easy to sew on a machine
- should be lightweight but not see-through.

Both specifications list requirements, making selecting fabric easier for the designer who must choose a fabric which best meets the needs of the project.

B *Both these items started with a fabric specification*

Activity

1 Write a five-point fabric specification for the following items, then ask a partner to read each of them and name a suitable fabric, using the fabric table on pages 34–5:

a child's soft toy

b pair of fashion trousers

c summer dress

d winter coat

e cushion cover.

Ask your teacher to check your fabric choices.

Summary

Properties and characteristics of fabrics play an important role in fabric choice.

You must consider all constraints and needs before making a fabric selection. Using a specification helps.

A designer has an important role to play in fabric selection, but it may be the manufacturer or customer who has the final say.

Remember

Fibre content is not a fabric name!

2.2　Labelling

What is on a textiles label?

All textile products (any product with 80 per cent or more textile content) have to be labelled with a range of information to inform the customer about the product's care, safety, quality standard, size, fibre content (including percentage) and where it came from (country of origin).

With the increased demand for environmentally friendly products textile items may also have recycling labels, **eco-labels**, organic and fair trade labels.

Objectives

Learn about the legal requirements for labelling textile products and how this information informs the consumer.

⊘ links

See Moral issues, pages 76–77.
See Environmental issues and sustainability, pages 82–83.

A *A garment label showing legal requirements and other information*

Care labelling

Care labels must be included so that a customer can care for the product correctly; if a customer fails to follow instructions this can affect their consumer rights. For example, if you machine wash a wool jumper and it shrinks in size but the label says hand wash only then it is unlikely you will get it replaced if you take it back to the shop.

Soure **B** gives symbols and their meanings relating to care of a textile product.

Symbol	Meaning
Ⓐ	Normal textiles dry-cleanable in all solvents. A circle on its' own means the same as this.
Ⓟ	Normal textiles dry-cleanable in perchloroethylene, White Spirit, Solvent R 113 and Hydrocarbon Solvent.
Ⓟ	Textiles sensitive to dry-cleaning which may be cleaned with the same solvents shown for above but with a strict limitation.
Ⓕ	Dry-cleanable in White Spirit, Solvent R 113 and Hydrocarbon Solvent.
Ⓕ	Textiles sensitive to dry-cleaning which may be cleaned with the same solvents shown as above but with limitations.
⊗	Do not dry-clean. Be careful with spot removal.
⬚	Hot iron (210°c). Cotton, linen.
⬚	Medium iron (160°c). Wool, polyester mixtures, some silks, viscose.
⬚	Low iron (120°c). Acrylic, nylon, acetate, triacetate, polyester & silks.
⬚	Do not iron.
⊡ ⊠	1. Tumble drying allowed. Dots in centre indicate heating temperature. 2. Do not tumble dry.

B *Care labelling*

Quality and safety labelling

Textile products are often tested for safety and quality so the consumer can be confident in the product they are buying. These tests are carried out by either the British Standards Institute (BSI Kitemark) or to achieve the European Safety Standard (CE mark). These tests not only test the quality of the product but also the manufacturing process: the manufacturer pays for the test and if the product passes they can fix the **quality label** to their product. Children's products can undergo tests for safety, the Lion Mark for toy safety is a **safety label** awarded after testing by the British Toy and Hobby Association.

C *The Lion Mark*

Eco-labelling

In today's world it is important that manufacturers and consumers are aware of environmental effects on our planet, and the textile industry has to play its part. Consumers are attracted by eco-labels as they feel that they are doing their part to reduce adverse effects on the planet, and manufacturers are also under government pressure to conform to 'green' policies. Eco-labels can be awarded if a product uses an eco-friendly system to produce the product or the product is made from **recycled**, sustainable, **organic** and natural dye sources.

D *The European Eco-label*

Summary

Labels on textiles are for informing the consumer about how to care for the product, what it is made of, where it came from, its size, any warnings and what standard it has achieved.

Some labels show how environmentally friendly the product is and how to dispose of it.

Products and systems are tested and labels are awarded that will give the customer peace of mind, such as after standard testing and eco-testing.

Key terms

Eco-label: found on an environmentally friendly product; awarded because of content or manufacturing system.

Care label: label contains information on how to care for and maintain a product.

Quality label: given to a product that has passed a standards test for the quality of the item or the system by which it has been produced.

Safety label: shows the product has passed safety testing standards.

Recycled: a product that has been reused in some form.

Organic: produced using natural fertilisers, pesticides and herbicides to protect the biodiversity of the environment and workers' health.

⃝⃝ links

Find out more at **ec.europa.eu/environment/ ecolabel**, for information on the European eco-label.

See Health and safety: consumer rights, pages 86–87, for the BSI Kitemark and European Safety Standard mark.

Activity

Design a new labelling symbol for eco-friendly textile products. Consider one for a child's product, and also make it child friendly. You may want to research existing eco-label designs before you design yours.

AQA Examiner's tip

You could be given labels to identify in an exam, and care symbols to select for a fabric, so learn them well.

Dyeing

Dyeing textiles involves immersing or dipping a fibre, yarn or fabric in a colour pigment to change its colour. We have been doing this for centuries and will continue to dye fabrics for many centuries to come. Colour is known as a **pigment** and the way of keeping (fixing) the colour is to use a **mordant**, a chemical that fixes the dye to help prevent loss of colour when washing or wearing the product. To be successful at dyeing you must:

- achieve the right colour
- make sure the colour is fixed (often called fast) so it does not run or wash out
- make sure the colour is even throughout
- make sure the dye does not damage the fibre, yarn or fabric
- make sure you can repeat the process and match the colour.

Dyeing methods

Chemical dyeing

This is the method that uses pigment (chemical) dyes with salts added to fix the dye; these can be made up with water. The fibres, yarns or fabric are then immersed in the dye bath until the depth of colour is achieved. This type of dyeing can be done in the classroom or at home.

Natural dyeing

Natural and vegetable dyes were the first-known dye pigments and with the move to be more environmentally friendly are becoming popular again. These work best with natural and regenerated fibres and fabrics and require a mordant to fix them to the fibres. With natural dyes it is difficult to reproduce the exact shade each time.

Industrial dyeing

Industrial dyeing can be done at the following stages:

- **Fibre stage** – fibres are dyed in vats until the dye has penetrated the fibre to give good uniform colour and fastness.
- **Liquid polymer stage** – the polymer (artificial fibre) is coloured before extrusion so the dye is part of the fibre and gives excellent colourfastness.
- **Yarn stage** – dye penetrates well but take-up may not be as uniform as when dyeing fibres then making them into yarns.
- **Fabric stage** – this is quite a cost-effective method because manufacturers can hold undyed fabric and dye it when needed, depending on changing fashions and demand. Cross-dyeing, where two different yarns have been used, which take up the dye at different rates, gives patterned effects such as stripes and checks. Dyeing at the fabric stage is often known as piece dyeing, and the process can be batch (fabric pieces are held in the dye), continuous (fabric goes through dye pads and rollers) or semi-continuous (fabric goes through dye pads but is held for a time to set the colour).

A *Natural dyeing process*

Dip dyeing

Fabric is dipped but not immersed to take up some dye on only part of the fabric or more depth of colour on part of the fabric; then it may be dipped again to get two or more colours blending together. This can be done in the classroom and achieves a popular patterned effect.

B Dip-dyed yarn

C Tie-dyed fabric

Resist dyeing

In resist dyeing a piece of fabric is dyed but part of the fabric is made to resist the absorption of dye as necessary to give a patterned effect.

Tie dyeing

In tie dyeing the fabric is wrapped, tied or folded in sections to stop the absorption of the dye. The fabric is then put in the dye bath and left for the required time. A multi-coloured effect can be achieved if the fabric is untied after the first colour is set and then retied and redyed in a second colour. Items such as buttons and pebbles can also be tied in to get further types of patterns. The tie-dye effect is popular for T-shirts and soft furnishings.

Batik

Batik is the resist method of using melted wax, a flour mixture or gutta, which is applied to the fabric in patterns to resist the dye when dry. The item is either dipped into the dye bath or the fabric is stretched on a frame and dye is painted on to the fabric. Sometimes cracks appear in the resist giving a cracked effect. Silk and cotton fabrics are best for this method.

Tritik

This is similar to batik but the resist is made up of tightly pulled stitches instead of wax. Again this method works best with cotton and silk.

Shibori

This is a folding process, where dye is added to folded fabric, which is then steamed to set the dye. Unfolding the fabric reveals a sculptured effect.

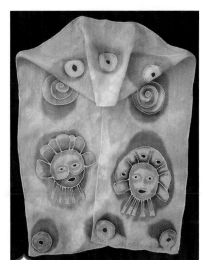
D Batik fabric

Printing

Printing is the method of applying colour to fabric to make decorative patterns in a uniform way. There are many printing methods available.

Printing methods

Block printing

This is a traditional printing method where a block made from wood, rubber, sponge or metal is shaped into a **relief** pattern (usually using a laser cutter or by hand), then dye is applied to the block and it is hand printed, or stamped, on to fabric. The print can then be repeated several times to achieve a pattern.

Screen printing

This method requires a screen, which is a frame with a fine mesh fabric tightly stretched over it. A pattern is either in stencil form or is blocked off on the screen itself, using a screen for each colour to be printed. Dye is pushed through the mesh fabric with a squeegee tool to evenly disperse the dye into the fabric below in the areas that have not been blocked out. Flat-screen printing is done in a similar way but machines operate each stage and often the pattern is applied to the screen digitally. Digital printing is a favoured method for small batches of fabric, as screen printing is an expensive process requiring space and specialist equipment.

Engraved roller printing

Engraved roller printing is an industrial method for large print runs; metal rollers are engraved with a pattern and dye reservoirs apply the colour as needed. As in screen printing a roller is needed for each colour; the method is therefore too expensive for short runs of fabric, but it can be very cost-effective for large print runs as hundreds of metres can be printed per minute.

Key terms

Relief: relief printing and dyeing means something is used to block the dyes from absorbing and is called a relief, e.g. string on tie dye or card on stencilling.

links

Find out more at
www.rocketfuelpress.com

E *Screen printing process*

Transfer printing

Transfer dyes are applied to paper and then heat transferred to the fabric. In school you can do this with transfer paints and an iron. These chemical transfer dyes are better suited to synthetic fabrics, on which they give a better depth of colour.

Stencilling

Stencils are made from card or acetate; the pattern is cut out and then the dye is sponged or brushed into the cut-out areas. Each stencil can be used several times. Today many stencils are made using computerised cutting machines for more accuracy than hand-cut stencils.

Digital printing

A design can be made on the computer using computer-aided design (CAD) packages and then either transferred on to paper (sublimation paper), which can be transferred to the fabric with heat, or it can be directly printed on to the fabric using a textile printer and then steam heated to fix the design. In direct printing the fabric may need to be thickened using a special chemical agent, which can be washed out afterwards, to help it feed through the printer.

F Digital printing

Summary

Dyes are either chemical or natural and both types require a mordant (fixative) to set them.

Methods of dyeing depend on the effect required and the type of fibre or fabric.

Patterns can be formed on fabrics using dyes, through relief methods or printing methods.

Computers are now an important tool to speed up and make the dyeing and printing processes more efficient.

Activity

Design a repeat pattern on A4 paper using the theme of 'Leaves'. Then use the equipment available to you in school to print your design on a sample of fabric.

AQA Examiner's tip

You need to be able to explain methods of dyeing and printing; using small, labelled sketches is always easier. Have a go at dyeing and printing yourself, as this is much better than just reading the explanation or watching someone else do it.

2.4 Fabric enhancement

Surface decoration

Dyes and printing **techniques** are not the only ways to get colour and pattern on to a plain piece of fabric. The following explains a few other techniques you may want to try. These techniques have endless possibilities for creating decorative effects.

Embroidery

This can be done by hand or by machine in a range of colours and patterns without giving too much of a raised surface. The fabric is still usually washable.

Appliqué

This technique is a quick and easy way to put a design on a piece of fabric by cutting out fabric shapes and sewing them to the background, by hand or machine. The shapes can be hand tacked, glued or fused into position to help with accuracy. This is a popular design enhancement method for children's products.

Quilting

This is a layering technique often used to add insulating properties to products. This uses an outer fabric, an inner soft padding and an under-lining fabric, which are stitched in a pattern either by hand or machine to create texture, pattern and warmth. Quilting is used for clothing, home furnishings and upholstery products.

Beading, sequins and other components

Beads, sequins, buttons, diamanté, pearls, studs, etc. are usually added to enhance, add colour and texture, catch the light and give weight to products. The components are hand sewn, glued, heat transferred or machined to the fabric in patterns or all over. Hand beading is very time consuming and makes garments very expensive.

Patchwork

This is a traditional technique that is often used to recycle fabrics. Fabrics are cut into geometric shapes and then stitched together to create a pattern and a larger piece of fabric. Patchwork is traditionally hand sewn but this technique can be machined to speed up the process.

Manipulation of fabric

Fabric can be **manipulated** not just for fit or shaping of a product but also to add a decorative look to the product.

Pleating

This method requires the folding of fabric on the vertical length and, usually, fixing the pleat at one end with stitching. A tuck is where the

A *Appliqué design*

B *Quilting*

fold is held at both ends with stitching and is often horizontal. Pleats and tucks add decoration and reduce fullness. Skirts are commonly pleated. Some designers exploit the thermoplastic properties of synthetic fabrics and heat set pleats for a very creative effect.

C *Pleating*

D *Issey Miyake pleats*

Gathers

Gathers are small stitches pulled together to reduce fullness (length). Again these are common on the waistlines of skirts, but they are also popular on sleeves, yokes and hems to add volume (shape) to a garment. Elasticated thread (shirring elastic) can be used to gather parts of the fabric to improve fit and add texture and pattern. Smocking is a traditional method of gathering fabric to reduce fullness; the gathers are held with patterned embroidery stitches.

Darts

Darts are a method of reshaping a garment or product but they can also be decorative if stitched on the surface (rather than inside the item), giving it textured flaps.

Heat setting

Heat when applied to fabrics can change the texture and shape but it is important to be aware of the fibre properties so that heat is used effectively. Heat and moisture and agitation applied to wool will felt it; heat applied to polyester or polyamide can soften it and when the fabric is cooled set in pleats and crinkle effects.

Textured effects

Distressed effects such as brushing, shredding, fraying, sanding and stone washing are popular methods of creating decoration and aged effects on products.

Summary

Decorative techniques can add colour and texture, reduce fullness and enhance a product.

Manipulation of fabrics means folding, twisting, pressing and stitching to change the shape, reduce fullness and add interest.

Key terms

Technique: a method used to add a feature to a fabric.

Manipulated: moving fabric by hand to shape or position folds or when a fabric is moved, folded, stretched or handled to change its look, fit and texture.

Distressed: the way a fabric has been damaged/changed from its original state to give texture, colour or an aged look.

∞ links

Find out more at www.isseymiyake.com or www.pocketmouse.co.uk/cgs3pg.php

E *Smocking*

Remember

When selecting an enhancement effect you have to consider the end use of the product. Will it be a suitable effect for the user?

Activity

Get four pieces of calico 25 cm x 25 cm and have a go at adding texture using a manipulating technique, then add decoration using stitching and/or components to at least one manipulated sample.

AQA Examiner's tip

Make sure you can explain some decorative techniques in a step-by-step flow diagram as this may help when you are tested.

3 Components

3.1 Fastenings

■ What is a fastening?

A fastening is a component used for closing products for fit, security, or for enhancement. When choosing a fastening a designer must consider the following:

- What product is the fastening for and what would suit it?
- What role does the fastening have to play in the product?
- How secure does the fastening need to be?
- How much will the fastening cost?
- Does it need to be a design feature?
- Does it need to be invisible?
- Can it be manufactured?

■ Frequently used fastenings

Zip fasteners

Zips are one of the most secure fastenings, and reasonably quick and easy to apply to products. There are different types of zips, which come in different weights; some are nylon and some metal. The weight is chosen to suit the fabric weight as well as matching the colour, and metal zips are used when strength is required (such as for jeans). Zips are fixed on tapes often made from woven cotton, polyester and polycotton.

Other types of zips include:

- fixed end (base of zip)
- open ended (for jackets)
- **concealed fastening** (invisible)
- decorative (diamanté set)
- two-way (two runners up and down, e.g. for bags).

Buttons

Buttons come in a wide range of sizes and materials. Designers select the best material and size of button to fit the product and the way it will be cared for. A button can be damaged in the wash or dissolve in dry-cleaning chemicals. Most buttons are fastened with a buttonhole but some have loops. Buttons are not just to fasten but can also enhance a product through matching or contrasting the colour, or adding a feature by being shaped in an unusual way or being patterned. Some expensive products have fabric-covered buttons, matching the button to the fabric identically.

Objectives

Learn about the types of fastenings and their uses.

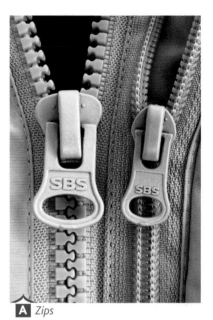

A Zips

Key terms

Concealed fastening: fastening that cannot be seen on the outside of the product. It can be hidden in a seam or by a flap of fabric.

B Covered buttons

Hooks and eyes

These are usually made from metal and are used when a flat fastening is needed. They can be hand or machine sewn in place and also come in tape form, giving a length of hooks and eyes, as used in underwear and corsetry. They tend to be black or silver in colour.

Velcro

Velcro is a hook-and-loop-style fastening used for quick, simple applications, especially for children's products, as it is safe and easy to use. It is not a suitable closure if the fabric is fine, as it is bulky and the hooks can snag finer fabrics. It washes well and is hard wearing but the hooks can pick up other fibres over time, making them less effective if not cleaned regularly.

C *A corset with hook and eye fastenings*

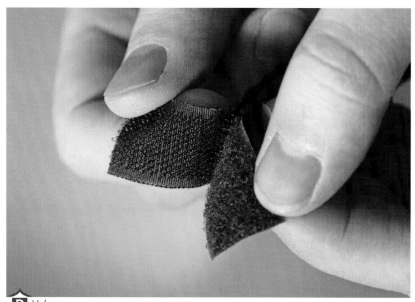

D *Velcro*

Press-studs

Press-studs or poppers are simple, flat closures used for many textile products. They can be metal or plastic and can be part of a design feature or just a cheap, simple closure. They need to be matched correctly and the size selected must be appropriate to the force that may be put on the fastening.

E *Press-studs*

Eyelets and lacing

Metal or stitched eyelets are placed on the product and laces are threaded through to form the closure. This can be decorative and can also allow for adjustment in the fit of the product. This style can be found in corsetry and dresses and on footwear.

F *Eyelets and Lacing*

Buckles

Buckles are popular as a fastening on belts, bags and shoes; they can be made from metal or plastic and can be very ornately decorated or very simple. Buckles often have eyelets to fasten into or you may just fold the fabric in a sliding action to tighten or loosen. Modern buckles can have LED components with lit-up names on the buckle.

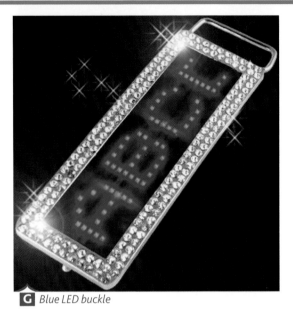

Toggles

Toggles are similar to buttons but tend to be cylinder shaped and can be wood, metal or plastic. They require a loop or cord to fasten and some modern toggles have a tightening spring-clip action to hold them in place. They are often seen on duffle coats or rucksacks.

H *A ski jacket toggle*

Drawstring

Drawstring fastening comprises a cord and an open channel to thread the cord through to tighten and close the product. Drawstrings are popular on coats, jackets, waistbands and bags.

links

Find out more at
www.unionfasteners.com

 *Drawstring bag*

Key terms

Drawstring: a type of fastening; also a way to reduce fullness in a product.

Activities

1. Find as many different products as possible and look at the chosen fastening. For each product suggest an alternative fastening and state how this might impact on the final outcome. Consider cost, security, style and care in your evaluations.

2. Design a range of fastenings for children's products including buttons, zips and Velcro style. Use the theme of the animal kingdom to inspire you.

Remember

Fastenings can be chosen for function or fashion in a textile product.

AQA Examiner's tip

You need to be able to name a fastening if it is shown in a picture or suggest an appropriate fastening for a product.

Summary

The fastening must suit the product, the end-user, the quality and the type of care needed.

A fastening can add aesthetic qualities as well as be a way to close a product.

3.2 Textile components

What is a textile component?

Components are extras that are added to the fabric used to make a textile item. Without components it would be very difficult to make textile items. Components are most often **pre-manufactured** (bought ready-made). Components can be home-made, such as shoulder pads or covered buttons. The role of components is to aid construction (threads), to allow for opening and closing (a zip), to add strength (**interfacing**), to embellish (beads), to **insulate** (wadding), to add shape (shoulder pads) and generally improve the quality of the product. When choosing a component a designer needs to consider care, cost, quality, aesthetic appeal, safety issues and end use. The following table lists some common components and their end uses, excluding fastenings.

Objectives

Learn what a textile component is.

Learn how to select a component for a product for the most effective outcome.

∞ links

See Fastenings, pages 46–49.

A *Components and their functions*

Component	Function	Examples
Sewing threads	To hold fabric pieces together, to add fastenings, to add decoration	Cotton, polyester, metallic and silk threads, stranded and pearl embroidery threads. Novelty threads (multi-coloured or invisible) and wool threads for knitted products
Beads and sequins	To decorate with colour and texture and catch the light. To add weight to a product	Plastic, wood, diamanté, metal, pearls and semi-precious stones
Ribbon, bindings, cords and braids	To add decorative edgings, or decorative features. To be used as ties, and fastenings	Fabric strips or different weights, patterns, widths and fibres. Bias binding will stretch when stitched on edges. Braids can have fringing, beads, feathers and embroidery added for decorative effect. Cord can be put into fabric casings as piped edge or seam
Interfacings	To aid sewing, add strength, give shape and structure, or to be used as a bonding glue	Non-woven sew or iron-on (fusible) fabric; paper backed or web-fabric bonding glue (Bondaweb)
Pre-manufactured motifs	To speed up decorative process and add a feature	School and team badges, children's animal motifs, etc.
Shoulder pads	To add shape and definition to the shoulder of a garment	Foam pad, can be fabric covered
Rivets	To add strength and decoration	Metal jeans rivets, diamanté, decorative rivets
LED bulbs	To add decoration, make visible in the dark and increase security	Used in footwear for children, on fashion belts and costumes
Boning	To add rigidity and structure	Used in strapless dresses, corsets and in underwear and can be plastic, rigilene or fabric-covered metal, steel
Elastic	To add stretch and reduce fullness to waists, cuffs, hems or stitched into the body of a garment or item	Tape in widths, shirring elastic thread, decorative waistbands and belts

Components and the future

As is the case with fibre and fabric technology, innovations in component technology are ongoing. The use of electrical components such as LEDs and fibre optics is still new ground for component design. The military have designed optic sensors that are put into soldiers' garments to detect harmful chemicals or warn them that the enemy has detected their presence. Thermal insulating wadding can be enhanced with temperature-regulation technology; these are known as PCMs (phase-changing materials) and are tiny microcapsules embedded in a wadding material. This means the wadding reacts automatically to a change in temperature. It is used in jackets to be worn where there are quick temperature changes, such as when skiing or for airport ground crew, and in boot linings. Inflatable technology is another innovation in component technology, enabling padding to be replaced with blow-up pads, for example in bras.

⃝⃝links

Find out more at
www.gossard.com

B *Components for aesthetics and function*

Activities

1. What are the functions of the components in the three products? (See Photo **B**.) Produce a table to show the components and functions.

2. What other components could have been used for a similar effect?

3. Why do you think the designer chose these components?

4. Design a school bag using a range of components for function and decorative effect. Label your ideas.

Key terms

Pre-manufactured: made ready to use in a factory.

Interfacing: an extra layer of material between the main fabric and the lining fabric.

Insulate: add warmth to a fabric to keep heat regulated.

Fusible: can stick to a fabric, using heat to fuse.

Summary

The component must suit the product, the end-user, the quality and the type of care needed.

A component can add aesthetic qualities as well as fulfilling its function.

AQA   Examiner's tip

You need to be able to name and identify a component. Questions will ask for reasons for your choice as well as for identification.

AQA Examination-style questions

1   (a)   Complete a five-point fabric specification for fabric to be used in a child's soft toy product. Give a reason for each point. The first has been done for you.

The fabric must be soft to touch.

Reason   Because it will be held close to a child's skin.   *(8 marks)*

   (b)   Describe in detail a fabric which could be suitable for the toy product and fits your specification.   *(4 marks)*

   (c)   (i)   Name one finish which could be applied to a soft toy fabric to improve its end use.   *(1 mark)*

   (ii)   Explain why this finish could be useful.   *(2 marks)*

   (d)   The toy manufacturer wants the fabric to be from a sustainable source; explain what this means and suggest a suitable fibre(s) for the fabric to be made from.   *(4 marks)*

2   A product is to be enhanced using a decorative technique.
   (a)   Name two decorative techniques that could be used.   *(2 marks)*
   (b)   Use notes and sketches to describe one of the methods named.   *(5 marks)*

3   (a)   Care labelling is an important part of a textile product.
   (i)   Name two factors that affect the information put on to a care label.   *(2 marks)*
   (ii)   What do the following symbols mean for the care of the product?   *(2 marks)*

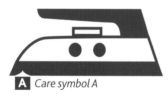

A *Care symbol A*

B *Care symbol B*

   (b)   Textile products can have labelling to identify other factors to the consumer; name four pieces of information that could be found on a textile product other than care label information.   *(4 marks)*

   (c)   A textile product is given the Fair Trade symbol, what does this mean? Explain.   *(3 marks)*

   (d)   Sometimes labels have components attached to them, why do manufacturers feel the need to include these extra components?   *(3 marks)*

AQA Examination-style questions

- Remember to learn the basics about fabric properties as these will be your points for choosing a fabric and your criteria for writing a fabric specification.
- You need to be able to describe how to do a technique; sketches that are annotated tend to be easier to understand.
- Your knowledge of labelling symbols is often tested, so make sure you know what they symbolise.

4

(a) Velcro® is a popular component used in children's products. Give three reasons why this is the case. *(3 marks)*

(b) Sewing Velcro® into a product to make sure it is functional and secure is an important technique. Write a five-point plan to describe how this may be done. (Sketches may be used to illustrate your answer.) *(5 marks)*

(c) A manufacturer does not want to use Velcro® in his new line of children's coats. Suggest two alternative fastenings that may be suitable and explain your reasons. *(4 marks)*

Design and market influences

In this section you will learn how to analyse textile products so that you can evaluate all aspects of design including use of materials and methods of working. Studying designs from the past and seeing the work of contemporary designers can inspire your own new, exciting design ideas and give you the information you need to make a successful product. You will learn why it is important to have a design specification to focus ideas and how to test a new product.

The following chapters will help you to consider the social, cultural, moral and environmental issues that influence textile design and manufacture. You will need to be aware of new developments in technology and current social issues to extend your subject knowledge and understanding. There is an increasing concern in our society to design sustainable products that have a low impact on the environment. This section will tell you about textile recycling, ethical design and organic cotton.

You will read about testing and evaluating during design development as part of quality assurance. The health and safety of those making and using the textile products must be considered during design and making. At the end of this section you will find out about the importance of labelling the product to inform the consumer and the risk assessments carried out by health and safety officers in the textile industry.

■ What will you study in this section?

After completing Design and market influences (Chapters 4–5) you should have a good understanding of:

- how designers get inspiration to make products
- how to analyse existing products
- product disassembly and the importance of taking a textile product apart
- design specifications
- the importance of quality
- testing, evaluating and trialling ideas and products
- the influences of social, cultural and moral factors and health and safety and the environment.

■ Activities

For each of the areas listed above, an exciting activity is suggested. The wide range of activities asks you to research, collect, examine, sketch, design, test, write and make. Some of the things you do can be presented for display in the classroom to help others learn from your work. Other activities ask you to find things out or to design and make, to help you learn more about textile design and market influences.

■ How will you use the information?

In Unit 1 (Written paper), you will be tested on your subject knowledge and understanding. You will need to show an awareness of how new developments in technology and current social issues, such as designing sustainable products, influence textile product design. In Unit 2 (Controlled assessment), you will need to design and make a creative and original textile product and demonstrate your textile skills and subject knowledge.

4.1 How designers get inspiration

■ Trend and colour forecasts

Designers need to know what consumers will want to buy in the future. This will ensure that the products that they are designing now will sell when they have been manufactured. To help them keep up to date with the next new ideas, they will attend trade fairs or look on fashion forecast websites to collect information about future fashions trends. New concepts or influences that will affect consumer preferences in the future are presented on a range of story boards that link to different **target market** lifestyles and consumer group identities or style images.

At the trade shows, manufactures present their new developments in fibres, fabrics and finishes, which they hope will inspire designers to incorporate their latest range of materials in the products that they are designing. Companies selling fabrics will be keen to promote sales by offering fabric swatches and specifications for the designers' reference.

Colour charts group exciting new colour combinations in easy-to-refer-to **colour palettes**, to inform designers of the fashionable shades for future seasons. These colour predictions have been researched by forecasters to help yarn producers work months ahead of the garment designers, and to develop fashion colour ranges into fabrics.

Objectives

Understand the influence of trend and colour forecasts on design ideas.

Consider how designers respond to a design brief.

Appreciate how visual research material can be effectively presented.

A *Trend forecast for Spring/Summer 2010 womenswear*

B *Manufacturers present their new fabrics to designers*

In addition to the use of fashion forecasts, modern technology has enabled a much more rapid response by designers to changes in fashion. Shop floor sales data and fashion influences from the media, such as what the latest celebrities are wearing, are directly determining product development. To some extent the traditional seasonal patterns of spring/ summer and autumn/winter fashion collections have been overtaken by a more flexible approach to product range development. Smaller mid-season additions to stock respond to the consumer drive for fast fashion.

■ The design brief

An individual designer or design team will work on a project that will lead to the development of a particular product or product range. The **client** will explain what is needed by setting a design brief. The brief will provide a starting point so that the designer can consider what will need to be researched in order to collect together information to guide design thinking. This early stage in the design process is known as **task analysis**. Once the brief has been understood and a plan of action noted, specific research can start.

The designer will need to research the theme and find out about relevant existing products. They will also need to consider the preferences of the target market and the purpose of the product to be designed. Appropriate textile materials, techniques and processes will need investigating and client requirements for costing, quality, company logos, health and safety, and issues such as sustainability may need to be taken into account. A simple **mind map** or a more detailed written report, such as the example in Student exemplar **C**, will outline the plan.

Key terms

Target market: also target group; the intended user/buyer.

Colour palette: also colourway; The colour or range of colours selected for the design of fabric or product.

Client: the person or company that employs the designer to design a product.

Task analysis: working out what needs to be done in order to respond to the design brief.

Mind map: also brainstorm or thought shower; a chart/ diagram listing thoughts/ideas as they occur. Words may be linked by arrows to show the thought process.

AQA Examiner's tip

During task analysis note down what you already know that will help you design and develop ideas.

Task analysis

Products

I will be looking at existing products in retail shops e.g. French connections, mango etc... to give me an insight on how a garment is manufactured and to give me some inspiration on design ideas. This will also inspire me on current fashions, colours and the different themes that are trendy this season.

Colours are very important; people want to buy a coloured garment that is the hottest colour to wear in fashion so they will look up to date. There are certain colours that represents different seasons and cultures for example, black is usually big in winter and yellow is usually big in summer. Therefore I should probably choose a colour that is ideal for the season and is most seen in catwalks, as most people tend to follow the fashion trends and I think this will make the product sell more. I will need to look at different themes and designs such as romance, the 60's and 70's fashion etc. in shops, which plays a big role on the attractiveness of a product. This will help me gather important information about the present themes, colour, patterns and designs in the high street market; customers would like to buy themes that is modern and in shops. I will also need to look at the construction of a product, this will benefit me on how to design and put my product together, so I will look at a range of clothes to find out the best ways to assemble my design.

To make the product more attractive and stand out patterns or decorative techniques such as embroidery, tie and dye, beading or appliqué are normally used on garments. They are usually used for finishing touches or for the main feature of the garment. I will be looking at existing products to give me an inspiration on the techniques they used. Choosing the right fabric for my product is very important; certain fabric can make the garment look expensive or cheap and tacky. There is a wide range of different fabrics such as cotton, satin, nylon etc... so I will need to decide carefully and compare which fabric will be suitable for my garment.

People

To enable me what my target audience prefer, I will be giving out 10 questionnaires in Selfridges about what kind of dress they would buy. This will give me the knowledge of what appeals to them e.g. which theme do they prefer, colour, cost, fabrics etc...so I can make a successful product.

I will also be asking people who work in shops about what kind of clothing recently have been popular. This will give me an idea of what product is appealing to certain age groups.

For further research, I could also ring up or write a letter to companies to enquire them about manufacturing and industrial processes to help me look further on to making my product.

Places

To inspire me and help me gather ideas for my garment, I will be looking at existing products in Oxford and Regent Street that have a range of high street shops such as French connections, warehouse, all-saints etc... this will give me an idea of what are the latest trends, colours, themes and how designers put an garment together. I will also visit the cloth house, which sells a wide range of fabrics such as cotton, linen, satin etc... or man made fabrics such as nylon so I will know which fabric is suitable for my product. I will need to look at components such as zips, hook and eye that is suitable for certain fabrics.

There are other sources e.g. Internet, libraries etc... where I can gain useful information that is similar to my idea. I will be looking at different techniques on how to sow a garment, the present fashion trends and the styles from different cultures.

Celebrity styles are very popular and influential because people want to dress like them to achieve the "celebrity" look. Additionally, I will look through catalogues and fashion magazines that will inspire me, give me some style tips, and I will collect images from top designers that can relate to my project.

Processes

I will be looking at different industrial processes on how to construct a garment. There are different types of production system such as batch production; mass production etc... that I could use to manufacture my garment, so I will need to look at it individually and carefully make my final decision to see which one is right for my product.

To help me gain knowledge on how a product is sewn, I will need to research the different type of techniques and the best ways a garment can be put together as there are various style and width of stitches (normal or zigzag) to use and certain areas such as the straps of a dress is sewn. This will give me a plan of how to design my product.

I will need to find a suitable material I could use to manufacture my product. There are loads of different types of fabric I can choose from, so I will need to research which one will be right fabric for my product. This is important because every fabric have different properties; some are heavy, lightweight, stretchy etc... and if the material irritates the skin, it is likely that customers won't buy the product. Therefore I will need to choose a fabric that is comfortable and doesn't itch towards the skin. I will compare and test out the material that I could use on my product. This will help me to achieve a professional look.

 Jenny writes a more formal task analysis to explain her plan for research

■ Mood boards

During research, the designer will collect a wide variety of pictures and samples based on the theme. This material needs to be displayed on a single sheet to convey the essential ideas about colours, patterns, shapes and textures to inspire the design ideas. The most effective mood boards will clearly summarise the theme with a limited selection of inspirational and informative items. Mood boards can be compiled using a computer for speed and ease of communication with the client.

Mood boards are:

- a focused presentation of selected visual research material
- an inspirational display to capture the mood of the theme
- images, colours, fabrics, photos, patterns, textures and text arranged to express the qualities and concepts of the theme
- a means of communicating ideas to the client
- a way to inform and inspire design ideas, sketches and modelling
- sometimes referred to as theme boards or story boards.

∞links

Find out more at **www.wgsn-edu.com** for up-to-date fashion news, including colour and trend forecasts. This website serves the fashion industry but you may also be able to access this site using a student pin number from your school.

See use of ICT to design and present, pages 122–123, to find out how ICT is used to create story boards.

D *Mood boards focus ideas and inspire designers*

Activities

1. Compile a mood board based on the theme of 'Once upon a time …' to include a variety of textures, colours and patterns from pictures, fabric samples, magazine cuttings, etc. Summarise the mood in a few carefully chosen words and add text to the board using appropriate text colour and font style or handwriting.

2. Test the results. Does the board convey the theme? Could you simplify the display to make it more effective? Could a designer sketch exciting design ideas based on the information presented? Ask an expert's opinion.

Remember

Plan to carry out only essential research. If required, further research can be carried out at a later stage in the design process.

E *Steph's moodboard*

Summary

Designers refer to colour and trend forecasts to keep up to date with future fashion trends.

The brief is analysed in order to plan what needs to be researched.

The mood board conveys the inspirational theme.

4.2 Analysis of a product

Existing product research

Designers research existing products to see how other designers have coloured, shaped and styled their products. They examine which fabrics and components have been used, which decorative techniques have been employed and how the item has been constructed. Size and special features can be noted and labelling, price, quality and packaging considered. The designer may have access to sales data for the product or may use it to test the opinions of the target market.

In Student exemplar **A** a student designer, Sylvia, has made notes about existing products that her target market would buy. She has used the research to help focus her own ideas about designing a T-shirt to be sold in the Tate Gallery Shop. She has a clear idea about who will buy her new designs and has considered how they will compete with existing items in the shop.

Objectives

Understand what can be learnt from looking at existing products.

Consider the impact of special design features on the success of a textile product.

Identify the essential purpose of a product.

Aim: To analyse existing products in detail to get ideas about the information/ features that are needed for my product and what is currently on the market

Gilbert & George T-shirt (small)..

Good points:
* It can be worn by male or female because it is inspired by an artwork (Deatho Knock).
* The colours are contrasting so you can tell what the designs are clearly. eventhough it is just black prints.

Bad points:
* The neckline look too small, might not fit through the target audience's head with ease.

Possible modifications:
* increase the size of the neckline for the older target audience (25) to fit through with ease.

My Target Audience:
Young people who visits/participate in the Young Tate organisation in the gallery - aged 13-25

Description of the Product:
This tshirt is made from 100% white cotton. The detail design is in black which is in the inspiration of the artwork "Deatho Knock" by Gilbert & George. The background, which looks like a grid, has images of insects, plant life and also two soldiers fighting - holding swords and shields. This tshirt is sold for £30 in the Tate shop, in a range of sizes.

http://www.tate.org.uk/servlet/ViewProduct?id=31994

A Sylvia analyses existing products

B The baby learns about colours, shape, textures and patterns

Designing for a purpose

Textile products are made for a very wide variety of purposes, for clothing, accessories and furnishings and also for use in industrial, medical, architectural, landscaping and transport contexts. What guides the designer's thinking is the function that the textile product will need to perform, who it will be used by and how to make it stand out from similar existing products. The new product design must meet the client's specifications and be attractive enough to appeal to those making planned purchases or impulse buys. Understanding what is required will focus the design ideas.

In Photo **B** the baby clasps the toy, learning through exploring the colours, shape, textures and patterns. The toy's function is to interest and educate the child, and it must appeal to both child and parent.

In Photo **C** the reflective fabric in these garments is essential to the safety of the wearer. New technology is incorporated to give the product enhanced performance, to incorporate electronic components and to conform to safety standards.

C High-visibility life jackets keep child and pet safe from danger

Activities

1. Take a simple pair of jeans and look at them closely. Note the main features such as the shape, pockets, the small metal rivets that strengthen the seams, the zip opening and stitching detail.

2. Now consider a particular type of person – the target market – who would buy a pair of innovative fashionable jeans. Consider their interests and lifestyle, perhaps leisure, sporting or medical needs.

3. Design a pair of jeans to appeal to this target market. They might include electronic components with touch-sensitive fabric control panels and/or fabric that changes colour, lights up or releases a scent in response to a change in the environment. Health monitoring or safety features could be incorporated to receive, store or transmit data via built-in sensors, a keyboard display or global positioning system (GPS). Be imaginative and creative in your thinking. Label the drawing to explain your ideas.

∞ links

Find out more at **www.oneill.com** – view exciting fashionable products for outdoor wear.

See Fabric construction: woven, pages 24–25, and textile components, pages 50–51.

Remember

The most successful aspects of existing products can be incorporated, as appropriate, into a new design.

AQA Examiner's tip

When analysing textile products, link your written comments to the target market, function, marketability and aesthetics of the item.

Summary

The designer should be clear about the needs/wants of the target market in order to develop a successful product.

Inspiration and information can be taken from examining the work of other designers and existing, similar products.

4.3 | Product disassembly

Research using disassembly

Designers take an interest in a wide variety of textile products seen in daily life as well as those that are specifically researched for a project. They will note fabrics, finishes and decorative techniques, which create colour, pattern and texture in the product, and the components selected for appearance as well as function and performance. Designers also examine how the product may have been assembled. They consider the probable order of putting together the separate pieces to make the item and how special design features may have been added.

To help understand how a textile piece is made, each section of the item is examined closely, or it may be scrutinised and actually taken apart. Both methods are known as **disassembly**.

Disassembly is a very useful research method. It not only gives designers some good ideas to try out but also helps build up their understanding and knowledge of textiles.

Taking a textile product apart – how do I get started?

You will need:

- small, sharp scissors
- seam ripper
- iron
- ruler
- sketching equipment or digital camera.

The method is as follows:

- Record the front, back and inside close-up views of the product, as appropriate. This could include packaging, if new. Make written notes.
- Unpick the main seams, cutting the stitch but not the fabric. Remove care labels and any lining sections. Record and make notes about how each main section was joined, the type of seam and if there is a hem.
- For each section, unpick the additional parts, such as pockets, belt loops, interfacing and trims, fastenings, labels and other components. Note possible methods of adding these details and record results.
- Identify colouring methods and decorative techniques and at which stage they were applied. For example, try and work out if colour is added to fibre or yarn or during fabric construction, or by dyeing the fabric. Or, is the colour printed, painted, stitched or bonded on to the fabric? It can help to refer to books or the internet, or ask an expert to help you to understand how the product has been made.
- Present your researched information to explain how the product had been made. Label the photos/sketches with detailed **annotation** to record the results of disassembly.

Objectives

Identify materials, techniques and processes seen in textile products through disassembly.

Understand how appearance, function and performance of a product are linked to choice of materials and methods of manufacture.

Key terms

Disassembly: examining closely, unpicking seams and taking apart to reduce the product to its cut-out pieces of fabric and components.

Annotation: written labels and notes.

Vivienne Westwood

A major exhibition displayed the fashion collections of the designer Vivienne Westwood from her very early pieces to her latest designs. It was clear from seeing her lifetime's work that, as she gained knowledge and understanding of textile techniques and processes, her garments became more technically detailed.

Notes from the exhibition described how she gained inspiration and information about manufacturing techniques and materials from looking at historical paintings of costumes and from disassembling historical corsets. As a designer she is well known for her creative corset designs, which are inspired by past eras.

A *Vivienne Westwood incorporates historical techniques into her corset designs, such as boning methods to shape and support the garment style*

■ Developing a pattern from disassembly

The fabric pieces that result from taking apart a product can be laid out on paper and drawn around to make a new paper pattern. This can be the actual paper pattern, or the basis for pattern modification/ development, for a new product.

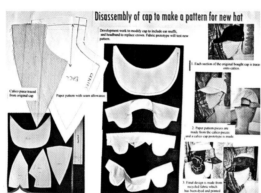

B *A plain canvas hat is disassembled to make a pattern for a new fashion product*

∞ links

Find out more at **www.viviennewestwood.com** – view the latest fashion collections and historical information.

Activities

1 Find an unwanted fashion accessory, furnishing item or piece of clothing, such as a young child's pair of dungarees. Examine the piece to work out the stages of decorating and constructing the piece.

2 Now sketch the item from various viewpoints, including an enlarged drawing of any very detailed parts. You could record the information using a digital camera instead of sketching. Label the disassembly work with written notes to explain what you have discovered through the close examination of the product.

Remember

■ When you have taken a product apart, iron all the fabric sections to unfold hems and seams to see clearly the shape and size of each separate piece.

■ The care label and swing tag will give you information about the product's fibres and fabric.

AQA Examiner's tip

When annotating disassembly drawings or photos explain the reasons for choice of material, technique or process involved in the manufacture of the product.

Summary

Disassembly will inspire and inform design thinking, building up a designer's knowledge and understanding of textiles.

Disassembly will save time when developing ideas, because designers can look at existing solutions and modify them to make new products.

Writing a design specification from research analysis

Once research data have been analysed, the designer is able to write a list of specific points to refer to when designing. These criteria will guide and focus ideas, ensuring that sketches, sampling and modelling are relevant to the design brief and to what has been found out during research. This list is known as the design specification.

What to include in the design specification

The design specification will outline the specific requirements for the new product:

- The function – for what purpose and for which target market?
- Performance – how will this influence product safety and quality? What modern and smart materials are to be featured?
- Special design features – what will make the product unique and appealing?
- The appearance – what colours, textures, shapes and patterns are suggested by the theme?
- The budget – what restraints are there?
- Are there requirements to consider such as social, moral, **ethical** or environmental issues?
- Materials, techniques and processes – are particular fabrics, decorative and construction methods to be featured?
- Size, shape and style will depend on target market, theme, costs.
- Aftercare – has the client specified instructions? Will this influence design ideas?
- Lifecycle – how long should the product last? How will it be recycled?
- Packaging – will this impact on product design? Will sustainability issues be considered?

Other types of specifications

When sourcing fabric, the designer will need to consider fabric characteristics, properties, quality and cost. These will be listed in the fabric manufacturer's fabric specification.

A **product specification** describes the product. An example can be seen in Student exemplar **A**. This lists the details about the tent so that a potential customer can decide whether it is suitable for their purposes.

The **manufacturing specification** for the tent would include instructions on the making of the product.

Activity

Look at Source **B**. For which target market was this range of products designed? What else do you think was taken into consideration by the designer of this item? Write a bullet point list to show what might have guided the design thinking of this student's work. This list is the design specification.

AQA **Examiner's tip**

When writing the design specification, focus on design criteria that are relevant to the product design, its purpose and target market.

Key terms

Ethical: according to moral values.

Product specification: describes the prototype or final product. It includes photo/working drawing, fabric and components, stitching and techniques information, size/measurements, care label and costing.

Manufacturing specification: describes the stages of manufacture and materials needed in order to make the product.

Specification

Below shows a list of what I will need to include for my design

Target market
My target market is for 18-24 year old women. It should create an elegant image that is attractive and is suitable to my user. I have researched my target audience's preference by producing a questionnaire and a market research to help me design my product. So combining both results together, I can produce a garment that will be appealing to my target audience and will hopefully sell successfully.

Packaging
Once my customers purchased the dress, I will be using tissue paper to wrap around the dress so this will prevent any creases and damages on the beads. The dress will be then placed into a paper bag so the customer can carry it around.

Aesthetics
The appearance will be a strapless cocktail style dress, which is suitable for an eveningwear. From my research, colours are bright and bold such as purple, yellow, and red and blue were the most popular colours this season. However from my questionnaire, my target audience prefer black, which is a sophisticated colour. However, I think they preferred black because it is normally a safe colour to wear. I have decided to choose bock or bright colours because in my other research, bright block colours seem very trendy this season and it is a young colour to wear. The fabric will be plain with a small decoration on the dress as what my target audience preferred.

The shape of the dress will be either flared or straight with a fitted bodice. The length of my dress will be just above the knee or on the floor and will have a sweetheart neckline. I will be using a zip at the back of my dress. I will be using beads and sequins for the decoration of dress.

Weight
I don't think it really matters if the product is light or heavy. As long as the product is comfortable and it doesn't put pressure on the customer's body.

Cost
From my questionnaire, my target audience have chosen £41-50 as an affordable price. Therefore I will use this price to calculate the maximum price I could spend on my materials and fabrics in order for me to make a lot of profit. I have calculated that I can only spend a maximum of £15 on my components and fabrics so this will control my spending money to prevent me from going over my budget.

Time scale
In my coursework, I am only allowed a limited of time to complete my project, which is 40 hours to make my garment. Therefore, the best way to use up my time carefully, I have produced a GANTT chart to estimate how long it will take to complete each stage of manufacturing the product.

Materials and Components
I will need to decide what type of fabric I will use to develop my dress carefully as some fabrics are very expensive such as silk. I don't have a specific material in mind but I have a few possibilities I could use for my dress. Dupion silk was my first choice because it is a strong and smooth material, which is highly suitable to use on my dress. However, the disadvantages are that it is quite expensive and is dry cleaned only. My second option was satin, because it is smooth against the skin, shiny and looks expensive. This material is also not that expensive to buy, thus I might use satin as my main fabric for my product.

Since my target audience preferred either an embroidery or plain dress, I have decided to design an embroidery detail on the dress because adding detail to the garment will add attractiveness to the product and may increase the price range to increase profit. Therefore I will be using beads and sequins in my design.

Size
The size of my dress will probably be a size 8, which I think is an average size. I also picked this size because most of my target audience is a size 8.

Green issues
The common way to recycle a material is to send it to the charity shop which is a popular way to recycle products. Another way to recycle products is to reuse it for a different purpose.

The carrier bag that I will provide for my customers to carry the dress will also be recyclable bag so this will improve the environment.

Special Characteristics
When decorating my dress, I will be using a embroidery design to make it look attractive as this is what my target audience preferred. Also, I am going to include a clothes label so this will make my dress look professional.

Durability
The dress should be handled with care to increase the life expectancy. So I will provide a care label for the customer so they will know how to care for the product properly. This mainly depends on the fabric used because every material has different characteristics; therefore most fabrics are handled differently.

When sewing in my beads and sequins, I will also make sure that it is sewn in high quality, to ensure that it will increase the durability of the garment.

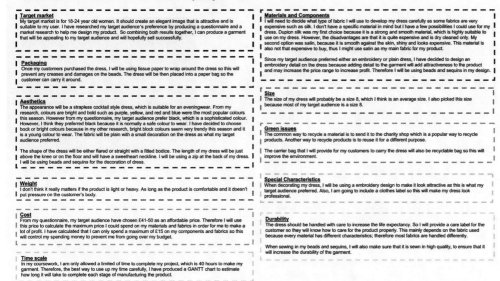

A *Jenny presents her design specification for an evening dress*

B *Sylvia designs a T-shirt for the Tate Gallery Shop; inspiration is drawn from the artists' work in the galleries*

C *Product specification for a mountain tent*

∞ links

Find out more at **www.tate.org.uk** – look at 'shop online' to search for textile products inspired by artists' work.

See Fabric choice and specification, pages 34–37, and Manufacturing specification pages 114–115.

Summary

A design specification lists points to be considered when designing.

Designers select appropriate fabric by referring to fabric specifications.

The product specification refers to the prototype while the manufacturing specification summarises the making of the final product.

Remember

A design specification should be written as a bullet point list to make it easy to read and to test ideas against.

4.5 Quality assurance

■ A quality product

Companies have to plan for quality throughout design and making activities. The client and end-user of the product have expectations that must be satisfied to make the product successful. A safe product, appropriate for use as intended, with appealing aesthetics, at the correct price and made to the agreed standards, will be a quality item.

How can quality be assured?

A total quality management (TQM) system is used to make sure that quality is designed and manufactured into the product. Every company employee has the responsibility to check they are following correct procedures to the highest standard. This chapter concerns the design stage of **quality assurance.**

To assure quality, at each stage of the design process, ideas are evaluated against the specification and kept focused on the brief. It is essential to understand customer preferences and market needs. Sampling, modelling and prototyping will check that materials and processes are safe and result in the correct quality. Testing and evaluating at this stage leads to modifications, improvements and further development. The final sample or **prototype** becomes the reference sample and this is the standard product that others in the production run can be checked against.

Objectives

To appreciate the importance of assured quality to company reputation.

To understand how product quality can be achieved through design development.

○○links

Find out more at **www.bsieducation.org** – look at the education section for ages 14–19 to find out more about standards for textiles products. See Quality control, pages 118–119.

Key terms

Quality assurance: the guarantee that the product is a quality product.

Prototype: the first trial product made to test materials, techniques and processes.

- Testing and modification of design ideas.
- Effective research and research analysis.
- Use of effective company organisation and management systems.
- Training the workforce.
- **Start sub-assembly**
- Prompt delivery of goods.
- Use of clear specifications.
- Monitoring raw materials, resources and production, feedback from quality control checks.
- Use of standards to check against and handbooks to explain procedures.

A *Product quality assurance framework*

CE mark and British Standards Institute Kitemark

B Sylvia samples techniques to test the suitability and effectiveness of stencil printing

Why is quality important?

A quality assured product will promote the reputation of the designer, manufacturer and retailer and is important to brand image. The client needs to feel confident that the batch of products made will sell and that their success will help build future sales. The statutory rights of the customer need to be upheld, and the product should conform to relevant standards to achieve the BSI Kitemark or CE mark. In short, the product must fully meet expectations and requirements.

When quality and safety symbols appear on packaging they assure customers that safety checks have been carried out on the product and during manufacture, and that the company and product have been awarded the mark of approval.

Remember

Quality assurance is the guarantee of quality that the manufacturer gives to the client and end-user of the product.

Activity

Examine swing tickets and other packaging materials of a range of textile products to find as many different symbols as you can that guarantee safety and quality. Make a collection of them with notes to explain what the symbols mean and to what sort of product they were attached.

AQA Examiner's tip

■ Be clear that you know how quality can be planned into the design process to ensure that customer expectations are met.
■ Understand the difference between quality control and quality assurance.

Summary

Quality is determined by a series of planned steps to test and monitor results during the designing and making of the product.

Quality and safety symbols on the product labelling and packaging are used to show the consumer that the product meets set standards.

4.6 Testing and evaluating design ideas

Testing and evaluation methods

To keep focused on the design brief it is helpful to check that ideas are relevant and appealing at each stage of the design process. This can be done in a number of different ways to help suggest improvements to the product design:

- testing design ideas against the design criteria listed in the design specification
- ideas shown to the intended users to collect feedback comments
- expert opinions sought to test appropriateness of proposed materials, techniques and processes
- samples and prototypes tested and trialled
- comparison of own product design to a similar existing product.

This testing is often carried out using questionnaires or interview questions that seek views about the performance, price and appeal of an idea or prototype.

Testing design ideas

Market surveys can be carried out to discover what consumers prefer and what type of new product might interest them. Special market research companies may be commissioned to collect the data, or a company might invite a panel of shoppers to give their opinions.

Experts will have excellent advice to give to designers about design ideas, methods of making and proposed use of fabrics and components. Photo A shows the work of a student designer, Stephanie, who is designing a fairy costume for a child actress to wear in a production of *A Midsummer Night's Dream*. She needs to know which idea would be the most successful product on stage, so she shows her ideas to an expert to get some feedback. Dawn Outhwaite, an experienced **costume designer**, is able to point out the best features of each design proposal.

Objectives

Understand how a range of testing and evaluation techniques can be used at various stages of the design process.

Consider how to make use of collected data to further design development.

Key terms

Costume designer: creator of clothing for actors to wear during filming or theatre productions. Design specifications will include set and stage requirements related to lighting effects, quick changes between scenes, and perhaps a series of the same costume for different parts of the drama.

Activities

1. Draw four or five different design ideas for an interactive dance mat using themes, shapes and colours that you think will appeal to young children.

2. Ask the parents of young children which idea they prefer and ask them to state their reasons. You could also ask their children which design they like the best. Before you talk to the intended users, jot down the questions that you need to ask, to find out about preferred colours, favourite theme, most appropriate size, etc.

3. Record your findings to show which idea is the most popular.

A *Stephanie seeks expert advice to test her design ideas*

∞ links

Find out more at
www.nationaltheatre.org.uk – you
can watch videos to find out about
the costume department and how it
operates.

Case study

Cuddledry

The 'Cuddledry' apron-style towel
for 'drying babies with cuddles' was
developed by two designers who
carried out user trials in order to
ensure the product was right and the
target market would buy the new
product. The designers appeared on
the BBC TV programme *Dragons'
Den* to present their product to the
team. The 'Dragons' were impressed
with the designers' testing and
evaluating methods and the towel is
now selling in 20 different countries.

B *Mothercare Cuddledry towel*

Remember

Testing and evaluating is an
essential part of product research
and development.

Summary

Opinions of intended users of the product and of experts, who may
design, make or sell similar products, will give valuable information
during testing and evaluation.

Further improvements can be made to the design idea and prototype,
as a result of data collected.

Testing the product prototype

Once a prototype has been made, designers need to check that their product:

- is fit for purpose
- is at the right price level
- has appeal
- includes appropriate materials and techniques
- has a low impact on the environment
- meets maintenance requirements
- is easy to manufacture.

A *A runner tests a new running vest*

User trials

The views of intended users can be collected by asking a sample of the target market to try out the product and record their opinions on how well it performed. A questionnaire could be used, an interview held, photographs taken or observations made in order to collect data.

Many companies are keen to get feedback from customers to check on the success of an idea for a new product and to help with further developments in their range of products. An example of this is seen in Photo **A**. With the increase in online shopping, customer reviews are also used as a marketing tool.

A student designer asks her target market to give their opinions about the success of her dress design. She tests against the design specification during the user trials and records the feedback in a **tally chart**. Her results, converted to percentages, are presented in Student exemplar **B**.

Objectives

Understand how user trials can test a new product.

Appreciate how results from user trials and product comparison can be used to modify and improve design ideas.

Key terms

Tally chart: a system to record the number of times something occurs; tallies are usually grouped into fives for speed of counting.

⚭ links

Find out more at www.nike.com – find out how this company tests the success of its products.

Activities

1 At home, carry out a user trial – you need to find a reusable supermarket bag made from fabric. Take sealed supermarket food packages and put them into the fabric bag.

   a Do the packages fit neatly into the bag?

   b Are the contents protected against being squashed, or knocked?

   c Is the bag stable when upright?

   d Is it easy to carry?

   Record your findings in a table or by taking photos using a digital camera.

2 Now make a table to note the results of your user trial; write a simple design specification in the first column of your table to help decide on the points to test.

3 From your conclusions you will be able to suggest some improvements that could be made to the original bag, such as a modification in shape or size, improved carrying handles or added design features such as a pocket. How could the bag's performance and appeal to the target market be improved?

Criteria	%	Result
Target market	100%	I asked my target market if they like the result of my dress and they responded very positive, they said that the dress is very attractive and appealing.
Packaging	100%	All of my users said that they like the idea of using a recyclable bag to carry the dress, as it will help protect the environment. They also said that the tissue paper was useful because it would help protect the dress.
Size	95%	The dress fitted all of my users; however some of my users fit better than the others. This may be because some people were from a different origin so they have different shape of body structure and measurements.
Aesthetics	100%	I received a very positive feedback about the appearance of the dress. They commented that the fabric look expensive and comfortable.
Cost	95%	The overall feedback about the price of the dress was a reasonable price. Some of my users suggested that they would pay a higher price for the dress because of the use of beading and the quality.
Materials and Components	92%	Some of my users said that the fabric is plain but the colour is very feminine and elegant. Everyone liked the embroidery detail on the waistband as it made the dress look more attractive.
Green issues	100%	I asked my users if they would be willing to recycle the dress by bringing it to the charity shop or use it for other purposes and they answered yes.
Weight	100%	My users commented that the dress is lightweight weight and it was not an issue. This shows that the dress was comfortable to wear and did not strain the user.
Quality assurance and design	94%	My users said that the quality of the dress is very good and the dress looked like it was brought from a shop. This illustrates that the dress is professional and it doesn't look tacky.
Durability	95%	One of my users agreed to wear the dress to her friend's birthday party for a day and came back with good results. "I did a lot of walking and dancing on that day and the dress was very strong and it didn't fall apart! It was very stable." This comment shows that the durability of the dress is strong.
Special characteristics	90%	I asked my users if hand washing the product was a problem for my users and they responded that hand washing the product was fine.
Suitability	100%	I asked my potential users if the dress was suitable to my users and the feedback came back with excellent results. They said that the dress is attractive and would attract many users.

B *Jenny carries out a user trial*

Product comparison

It is useful to test the prototype against a similar existing product to see how the new product would compete with others on the market. The new product should be an improved or updated version with a unique appeal to the target market. Analysis of results from product comparison will highlight the differences between what is already selling and what might be sold in the future.

AQA *Examiner's tip*

Make sure that you can explain the difference between user trials and product comparison.

Remember

The aspects tested by the intended user are based on the design specification, to see if the prototype product fulfils requirements.

Summary

Results from user trials and product comparison will guide the designer in making further improvements to the product, ensuring it meets the expectations of the target market.

Product function, performance and aesthetics can be fine-tuned to suit potential purchasers.

5.1 Social and cultural influences

Social change

New textile products are being developed to meet the needs of consumers and to appeal to their desire for up-to-date and fashionable items. Designers are often inspired to respond to changes in society (e.g. new ideas, technological advances and changes in the political and economic climate) and to world events.

In times of war, resources will be spent on funding the conflict, and materials for fashion products may be rationed or patriotic designs may be inspired. Technology may advance more rapidly in response to wartime requirements. For example, during the Second World War, nylon, a newly developed synthetic fibre, replaced silk in parachutes, as it was a cheaper fibre and would not need to be imported. It was also a popular new fibre for ladies' stockings, but was not readily available owing to wartime restrictions.

In times of plenty, consumers may have an increased disposable income to spend on fun clothing and home furnishings. As populations alter because of immigration, a new mix of people will bring their religious and cultural interests into society. The next generation will express their identity through new clothing and fashion designs. Gender issues may impact on design when the roles of men and women alter, perhaps with changes in types of employment and in the clothing needed for different workplaces. For example, trousers for females became more acceptable when they were worn by the women who worked on the land or in factories during the Second World War; afterwards they remained a popular item of clothing for women.

Now there is better healthcare and longer life expectancy, designing for elderly people and those with disabilities may be a future priority. As our society changes, designers respond to the latest issues and influences.

Objectives

Appreciate how changes in society influence textile product design.

Understand some cultural aspects that affect consumer demand for new products.

Consider how wearable electronics are being developed as society adapts to new communications technology.

AQA Examiner's tip

Be able to explain a wide variety of social and cultural differences that may have an impact on the design of a textile product.

Activity

Consider the needs of a young person with a disability who spends much of their day in a wheelchair. Design a fashionable textile product for this young person that features electronic devices. The new textile design should not only keep them stylishly warm and comfortable, but also provide entertainment and communication opportunities.

Draw and label your design ideas.

Fashion responds to society's search for the new

After the Second World War women desired feminine clothes that did not look like a civilian version of a military uniform and they were tired of the rationing, which had resulted in straighter styles with less fabric. In 1947 Christian Dior presented a fashion look comprising a fitted jacket with a nipped-in waist and full calf-length skirt, as seen in Photo **A**. Christian Dior's 'New Look' gave a very feminine fashion silhouette, with extravagant use of fabric. This new fashion was a great success because it responded to society's need to move on from the war years.

Today, **wearable electronics** are increasingly popular with those consumers who want communication and entertainment devices. New computer technology has altered the way people communicate and provides opportunities for entertainment from music, video and computer games. This has led to a rapid development in textile products that incorporate electronics, such as the O'Neill 'Hub' jacket and Bagir MusicStyle iPod tailored jacket.

A Christian Dior's 'New Look'

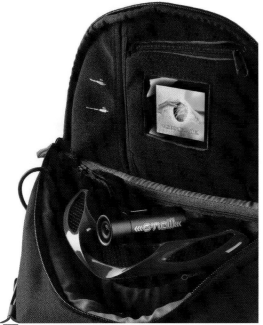
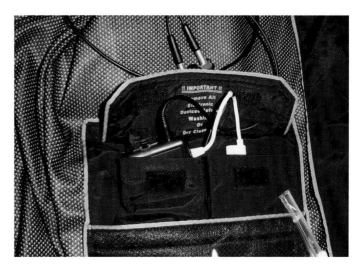
B These rucksacks incorporate electronic features

Photo **B** shows a range of innovative products. A solar panel charges the iPod battery in the backpack. Woven into the 'Hub' snowboard jacket are electrically conductive fabric tracks that connect the chip module to a fabric keyboard and built-in speakers in the snowboarder's helmet. The iPod provides entertainment while a Bluetooth device can control a mobile phone, with the microphone integrated in the collar of the jacket. Similarly, the tailored jacket in Photo **C** responds to the needs of a professional man who seeks stylish, wearable electronics in his workwear.

Key terms

Wearable electronics: electronic devices that are embedded into fabric or incorporated into clothing for sensing, monitoring, communication and entertainment purposes.

TAILOR MADE FOR MUSIC

Volume and selection controls for iPod sewn into fabric beneath left lapel

Wires linking controls to iPod run beneath lining of the suit

Pocket for iPod

C Bagir MusicStyle iPod tailored jacket.

D This jacket features a fabric keyboard panel on the sleeve

Military use

Society funds the development of new textile products for military use. One example of this is a soldier's glove called a 'Handwear Computer' Input Device' (HCID). Push-button sensors sewn into its fingers can act like a computer mouse. Sensors embedded on the back of the hand are used to activate radio communications, view and navigate electronic maps, and send commands. The glove can detect the movements of the soldier's command hand gestures to communicate with other soldiers. Some camouflage uniforms also feature toxic chemical detectors, micro-fuel cells and transmitters so that a soldier can be tracked.

Cultural influences on consumer choice

Within society some people may be restricted in their choice of textile products by their religious beliefs and customs. For example, Muslim women are encouraged to cover the head and body and so they often wear longer styles and head scarves. This is taken into consideration when designing for this target market.

Student exemplar **E** shows Esther's design for a hoodie for young Londoners; her design inspiration was taken from the London underground map and London postcodes. However, during testing she realises that the target market may be influenced by the conflict between inner city postcode gangs who may be too fearful to wear the hoodie. Social issues will influence the success of the new design.

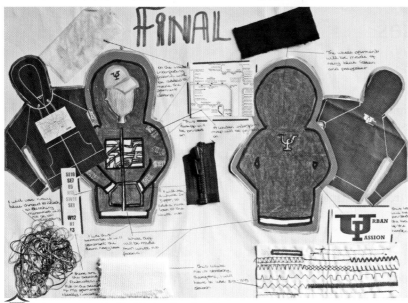

E *Esther presents the final design for a hoodie*

∞ links

Find out more at
www.vam.ac.uk – look at the
textile and fashion collections at
the Victoria and Albert Museum
in London. The social and cultural
influences on textile design of
different eras and countries can be
studied online or during a visit to
the museum.
www.fotosearch.com – see an
inspirational range of photos and
images of traditional costume.
See Textile components,
pages 50–55.

Traditional costume

Most countries have a traditional costume that may vary according
to the region within the country. The older generation might prefer
to see traditional clothing worn by all, but the increase in global
communications has influenced many younger people worldwide to
conform to a Western approach to fashion. Conversely, designers
are inspired by the traditional crafts seen in different cultures, and
fashion trends may be influenced by themes taken from a wide variety
of countries. For example, African, Asian and Oriental textiles often
inspire new fashion trends. In the photo below, Mexican textiles in vivid
colours could inspire a knitwear designer to develop a range of knitted
striped fabrics in bright colours.

F *Mexican textiles*

Summary

Textile product design is influenced by changes in society and reflects
the interests and values of the consumers.

Wearable electronics are used in fabric constructions that conceal
sensors and allow hands-free control of incorporated devices.

5.2 Moral issues

A fashion for ethical products

Many consumers are keen that fabrics and components used in the making of a product should be from a **sustainable** source. The current interest in buying **ethical** environmentally friendly products is a fashion trend but it is also seen as predicting a long-term change in the way people shop.

Many manufacturers are including **fairtrade** principles in their company policies to make their products appealing to consumers. They promote their textile goods using the recognised marks seen in Source A. When consumers see the symbol on product labelling they can buy the product, feeling confident that no worker has been exploited in the process of making it and that it is environmentally friendly.

A growing number of retailers are including ethical products in their ranges in response to consumer demand for **organic**, recycled and fairly traded goods. Also, some high street stores now include an ethical concession shop within their flagship stores. For example, People Tree, a well-known internet fairtrade clothing company, has a small concession shop in Topshop store on Regent Street, London.

Moral issues influence design

A responsible designer will ensure that design ideas are developed to make the product sustainable and will work with the client and manufacturer to apply fairtrade principles to the making of the product. Textile products are often made in less wealthy countries where labour costs are lower and perhaps factory health and safety regulations are less stringent, so it is important to check the stages in making to see if they conform to fairtrade standards. There has been much publicity about the use of child labour in textiles production in developing countries. Many consumers are upset by this exploitation and are keen to avoid buying products made by children. This target market would prefer to buy from companies that support their employees' local community through long-term commitment to pay fair wages and provide for the education of workers' children.

Ethical design is also concerned with the appropriateness of the product for its target market. This particularly impacts on children's products. For example, society generally agrees that designers should avoid making body-revealing sexy products for children, or those that include inappropriate printed slogans.

Animal rights' supporters believe that animals should not be killed to obtain their fur for fashion products. The Queen's Guards wear the iconic traditional fur hat made from Canadian black bears that are shot by agreement with the Canadian government. However, the British Ministry of Defence is testing new fabrics to find an ethical alternative that will replace the bear fur but allow the hat to keep its shape and repel water.

Objectives

Understand that moral issues need to be taken into consideration when designing textile products.

Understand what is meant by ethical trading.

Consider the influence of ethical issues on product development.

A Fairtrade mark used in textile product labelling to certify ethical trading and EU mark for greener products

B A knitted hat made in Nepal and sold by 'People Tree', a fairtrade company

C *These children are picking cotton, which may be grown using poisonous pesticides*

Activity

Use the internet to check the company principles of well-known high street stores and supermarkets. Look on the company website home pages and click on 'About us' to find out whether they list fairtrade and environmentally friendly policies for sourcing their textile products. For example, you could start with www.marksandspencer.com and www.sainsbury.com.

Case study

Black Yak

Black Yak is a fairtrade company, based in East Yorkshire, that sells clothing, crafts and accessories. The UK designers work with producers in the Himalayas, Nepal and around the world to make knitted and felted fashion products. Black Yak is a recognised and certified fairtrade importer of textile goods. The following principles are followed:

- fair price to producers
- equality in pay and working conditions
- safe working conditions
- long-term trading relationships
- health and educational benefits for the workers
- sustainable producer development
- a real alternative to poverty.

What type of person do you think would buy Black Yak products?

D *A Black Yak hat*

Remember

Consider moral issues when designing and developing your own textile designs.

∞links

Find out more at **www.ejfoundation.org/page141. html** to watch a video about the moral issues within the cotton growing industry.

www.labourbehindthelabel. org – learn about a campaign that supports garment workers to improve their working conditions, raising public awareness of moral issues.

See Environmental issues and sustainability, pages 82–83, for further details about designing a sustainable textile product.

See Health and safety: risk assessments, pages 88–89, to find out more about safe working practices.

AQA Examiner's tip

Be able to discuss specific consumer concerns about the sourcing of materials and the manufacture of textile products that may impact upon the success of the product.

Summary

Many consumers are keen to buy products that are ethically designed, made and traded and reflect the moral values of society.

Many manufacturers and retailers are including fairtrade principles in their company policies to make their products appealing to consumers.

5.3   Recycling textiles

Why is the recycling of textiles important?

There is a growing awareness of the depletion of the world's natural resources, and designers need to respond to society's changing attitudes to environmental issues. Textile companies are working to reduce the impact of textiles production on the environment. If designers and manufacturers source more fabrics and components from textile waste or pre-used textile products, then the need for newly manufactured materials could be reduced, saving energy and raw materials. There is a need to continue to reduce textile waste in **landfill** sites through recycling.

How are textile products recycled?

- Fabric off-cuts, roll ends, surplus and slightly damaged fabric are used by designers to produce unique pieces. This is an example of sustainability.
- Second-hand clothing is donated, swapped or sold to be reused by another person. Clothing banks, door-to-door collections and charity shops provide second-hand clothing to the high street and bales of clothing are exported to less economically developed countries.
- Garments and household textiles are deconstructed, and the fabric is reused. Vintage fabrics from the 1960s and 1970s may feature in a designer's fashion collection, or industrial wipes may be made from suitable cloth. Food sacks, lorry tarpaulins and items such as garden umbrellas are recycled to make unusual fashion bags etc.
- In fibre reclamation, woollen fabric is shredded into fibres for use in mattresses or as insulation material or for felting. The fibres can be re-spun into yarn.
- Plastic bottles are ground up and made into pellets, then melted and spun into polyester fibres for fleece fabric, or previously used polyester fleece is recycled into new polyester fabric.

Is recycling a new idea?

Past generations needed to reuse textile products or reclaim fabrics to perhaps overcome a shortage of available or affordable textiles. Expensive garments were often handed down in families from one generation to the next or from lady to maidservant: restyling and refitting to suit the new owner. Patchwork quilts made from scraps of fabric have traditionally recycled treasured remnants.

Textile recycling and fashion

Contemporary textile designers are inspired by the past to feature reclaimed fabrics and other recycled materials. These individual creative textile pieces appeal to some consumers who want sustainable or fashionable one-off products, while also influencing mainstream fashion. Many top fashion designers and textile students are exploring the idea of **customising** or **upcycling** garments or recycling materials. Many consumers will continue to demand **fast fashion** (as compared with **slow clothes**). However, the designer can ensure that

Objectives

Appreciate why textiles' recycling is important to society.

Consider how contemporary designers can respond to the increasing demand for producers of textile products to be ethically and environmentally aware.

A *Recycling symbol*

⏾links

Find out more at **www.patagonia.com** – look for product information. You can find out how this company encourages its customers to return their old fleeces to recycle into new garments. Patagonia's Common Threads Recycling Program is explained in detail.

biodegradable or easily recycled fabrics and components are specified for the fast fashion garments or that they can be designed for quick disassembly to lessen the impact on the environment.

Oxfam

The Gabrielle Millar dress for Oxfam in Photo **B** is colourful with exciting fabric contrasts. Traditional patchwork inspires this unique designer dress, which features the recycling of donated textiles. A number of top fashion designers, including Gabrielle Millar, Christopher Kane and Giles Deacon, were commissioned by Oxfam to showcase creative new pieces that incorporated reclaimed fabric to bring public awareness to Oxfam's work.

B Gabrielle Millar dress

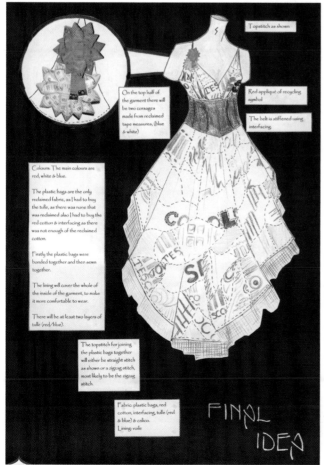

Topstitch as shown

On the top half of the garment there will be two corsages made from reclaimed tape measures. (blue & white)

Red appliqué of recycling symbol

The belt is stiffened using interfacing.

Colours: The main colours are red, white & blue.

The plastic bags are the only reclaimed fabric, as I had to buy the tulle, as there was none that was reclaimed also I had to buy the red cotton & interfacing as there was not enough of the reclaimed cotton.

Firstly the plastic bags were bonded together and then sewn together.

The lining will cover the whole of the inside of the garment, to make it more comfortable to wear.

There will be at least two layers of tulle (red/blue).

The topstitch for joining the plastic bags together will either be straight stitch as shown or a zigzag stitch, most likely to be the zigzag stitch.

Fabric: plastic bags, red cotton, interfacing, tulle (red & blue) & calico. Lining: voile

FINAL IDEA

C *Joanna explores recycling plastic carrier bags by bonding and stitching the plastic together and combining this with fabrics*

Key terms

Landfill: where waste is dumped and then covered over.

Customising: taking previously made pieces and transforming them into new designs by restyling or adding embellishments. Also known as **Upcycling.**

Fast fashion: fashionable clothing trend moving from catwalk to high street in record time; brief interest soon replaced by next fashion update.

Slow clothes: fashionable clothing that is bought, used and worn into the ground before discarding.

D *Hannah patches together recycled fabrics to make a fashionable corset-style top*

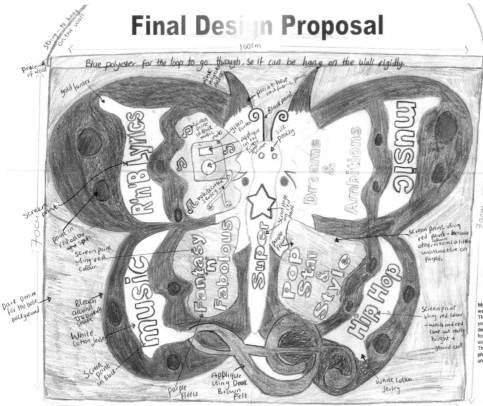

E *Ibrahim reclaims a wide range of fabrics to design a wall hanging, which features printed and appliquéd lettering on a 'dreams and ambition' theme*

Activity

Research

Research the fashion label 'Reclaimed to wear' by designer Orsola de Castro. From where does she source her fabrics?

See Link on Orsola De Castro.

Re-invent

Fight fast fashion by customising your own clothes. Select a garment that no longer fits you, or is damaged or outdated. A large T-shirt, for example, could be dyed, cut at the neckline, gathered at the sleeves with elastic and accessorised with embroidered badges. Decorate or restyle to re-invigorate your selected garment turning it into a new, creative one-off piece.

∞ links

Find out more at
www.fromsomewhere.co.uk – this company run by Orsola De Castro and Filippo Ricci makes individual fashion garments from unwanted top-quality fabric.
www.textile-recycling.org.uk – this textile recycling association promotes textile recycling and publicises its members' companies.
www.traid.org.uk – Traid stands for 'Textile recycling for aid and international development'. This charity's aim is to educate and to campaign for recycling.

Junky Styling

Case study

The company Junky Styling is well known for its quirky clothing made from deconstructed shirts and suits, as seen in Photo F. The company also offers a 'wardrobe surgery service'. This is like a professional customising of customers' favourite but outdated clothing to create a new, unique piece.

F *Junky Styling*

AQA Examiner's tip

- Be able to explain how fabrics and fibres can be reused to create new products.
- When answering questions, give examples of how particular designers or companies have created marketable fashion garments from recycled textiles.
- Learn the main stages in recycling plastic bottles into polyester.

Summary

People are increasingly concerned about the sourcing of textile materials.

Contemporary fashion and textile designers are creatively recycling to make limited-edition pieces.

Garments can be reused, fabric reclaimed, or fibres re-spun from recycled plastic or fabrics.

Sustainability

Many consumers are interested in green and ethical issues and are demanding sustainable products. 'Sustainable' refers to products that have been designed and made to have a lesser impact on the environment and improve the working conditions and economic security of those making the product. Responsible designers modify design ideas to ensure that sustainability issues are taken into consideration when making decisions about choice of materials and method of manufacture.

Product design and sustainability

A growing number of textile companies are adopting a company image that shows them as environmentally friendly and having ethical values, and many well-known retailers include an ethical collection in their product range. They recognise that consumers are increasingly 'keen to buy green'. This is a current fashion trend but also essential if the textile industry is to be sustainable in the future.

Sustainable product design will include:

- sourcing organic, biodegradable, reclaimed or recycled fabrics and components
- selecting fabrics that have been specially developed as sustainable
- developing a product that can be easily dismantled for reclamation and can be recycled
- designing a high-quality product with an extended life
- making use of modern, easy-care finishes, which reduce laundering requirements
- reduction of waste and pollution during manufacturing
- processing fabric without use of toxic chemicals, such as bleach and toxic dyes
- use of **renewable energy** to power machines, and increasing water efficiency during manufacture
- labelling products to inform consumers
- applying fairtrade policies, for workers' health and safety and for economic benefits
- careful consideration of location for manufacturing and method of distribution, to cut carbon emissions.

Labelling to promote sustainability

Many environmentally friendly products are clearly labelled to justify to the consumer why they are sustainable. Eco certification is necessary to identify a sustainable product and to detail a product's origin, place of manufacturing process and the scale of sustainability. This is still a developing area of the textile industry. Some current labelling can be seen in Photo **B**.

⚭ links

Find out more at **www.patagonia.com** – look for environmentalism for more information about sustainable product design. Patagonia's 'The Footprint Chronicles' is an interactive site and the impact of a product can be tracked through its lifecycle.
www.cbwt-learning.co.uk – find out about the wider effect of textile production on the environment.

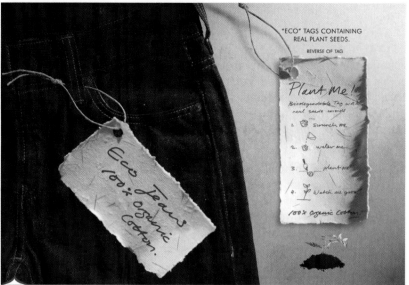

B *Soil Association organic standard*

A *Levi's Eco jeans are advertised to appeal to consumers who want an environmentally friendly product and one that is sustainable*

Levi's Red Tab eco jeans

The well-known denim jeans company Levi has developed eco jeans for consumers who will pay more for a pair of sustainable fashion jeans. The jeans are made with 100 per cent organic cotton denim and feature a coconut shell button on the waistband and uncoated metal fly buttons. Natural indigo dye has been used and a fabric finish has been produced from potato starch, mimosa flower and Marseilles soap. The jeans are produced in the Levi factory in Hungary following sustainable principles.

C *Levi's eco jeans*

Case study

Activity

Read the following, which lists the stages in the lifecycle of a standard pair of jeans from cotton field to landfill.

- Cotton plants are grown using chemical fertilisers, pesticides and herbicides.

- Spinning the fibre and weaving the basic denim fabric uses electricity generated by fossil fuel.

- Bleaching, dyeing and softening the denim fabric uses toxic chemicals and excessive water during processing.

- The jeans are sewn in a 'sweatshop' factory in a less developed country, where labour is cheap and working conditions unregulated. Lots of fabric is wasted during manufacture.

- The jeans are taken by air and road transportation, using oil, petrol and diesel, for thousands of miles to reach Europe.

- They are put on a supermarket shelf, packaged in plastic, in out-of-town stores, at a low price.

- They are washed after every wearing at 60 °C and tumble dried.

- Unwanted after three months, because of a tomato soup stain on the lower trouser leg, they are thrown out with the general rubbish.

Now rewrite the lifecycle giving it the title 'Green jeans – from organic cotton to customised fashion product'. Use the list on page 78 to help you describe the making of a sustainable pair of jeans and see Recycling textiles, pages 74–7, to remind you about recycling and customising.

Ethical fabric production

Organic cotton

Cotton producers often use synthetic chemical fertilisers to boost crop production, pesticides to kill off insects that will damage cotton crops and herbicides to prevent other plants from growing alongside and competing with the main crop. These chemicals increase productivity but can cause ill health and injury to cotton workers, and also traces of the chemicals can be found in the finished cotton product.

Organic cotton is grown without the use of such toxic chemicals. Many consumers prefer to buy organic cotton so that they are not contributing to cotton workers' health problems and to feel safe using the organic cotton product. In recent years the demand for organic cotton has dramatically increased, especially for baby clothes and accessories.

D *Organic cotton is a popular fabric choice for babies because of its safety, breathability and natural softness and colour*

Tencel – a modern fabric

Designers may choose to use a fibre such as Tencel, which is considered to have less impact on the environment than many other fibres. It is a regenerated fibre made from the cellulose found in wood pulp from sustainably grown and harvested trees, and the solvents and water used in processing are continually recycled. It is one example of a biofibre, but other plant materials can also be used to source cellulose, such as bamboo, sweetcorn and the soya bean.

Tencel is biodegradable, strong, soft, lightweight, drapes well and is breathable. Tencel is therefore a popular choice for a sustainable fashion garment. However, Tencel requires harsh chemicals to fix the dyes to the fabric so a fabric with natural colouring may be preferred, such as that made from a newly developed, naturally pigmented coloured cotton plant that does not require dyeing at all.

The dresses in Photo **E** are made from organic and sustainable textiles such as bamboo, soy, hemp, modal and tencel, together with reclaimed ends of fabric rolls. This young fashion designer creates ethically sound designs which appeal to those who wish to buy fashionable and luxurious garments.

E *Sustainable fashion by designer Feng Ho*

Summary

Textile designers and manufacturers are under social pressure to reduce the impact of textiles on the environment.

Careful use of raw materials and natural resources in textile production will ensure that they are available to future generations.

Textile technologists are continually seeking to develop new fibres that have improved performance and are sustainable.

links

See Recycling textiles, pages 78–79, for further details about reclaiming and recycling materials.

See Moral issues, pages 76–77, to learn more about ethical trading.

See Health and safety: risk assessments, pages 88–89, to learn more about safe working practices and environments for workers.

Labelling to inform the consumer

Consumers need to be confident that a textile item is safe to use and meets required standards. There is **legislation** to protect consumer rights. Labelling on the product and its packaging will provide the relevant information about:

- country of origin to say where the product was made
- fibre content, which will affect care instructions and product **flammability** and warn those allergic to certain fibres
- fire and safety warnings, such as product flammability warnings on upholstery, furnishings, soft toys and children's nightwear, and choking **hazards** for small children
- care and washing instructions
- British and European standard symbols, such as the Kitemark and CE mark
- trademarks to guarantee quality, and protect the manufacturer from copying by others and from cheaper imitations
- size
- product identification code
- environmental and ethical status.

The manufacturer will use symbols on the label to inform the consumer and promote sales. The consumer, however, has the responsibility to use and care for the product as instructed on the labelling.

The British Standards Institute (BSI) tests products and the process by which they are made. If the product is of the required standard then the manufacturer can display the BSI Kitemark on the product labelling. Consumers trust that products bearing the Kitemark have passed a rigorous certification process and will not only be safe to use but will also be fit for the purpose for which they were designed.

The CE marking is a mandatory European marking for textile products, such as those for children. The symbol shows that the essential health and safety requirements set out in European Directives have been met.

Companies may add their name and logo to the label along with a certification trademark, such as the Woolmark. This type of trademark can be used under licence, providing the product meets agreed quality standards.

Designing safe products

A designer must consider the needs of the target market and it is essential that a safe product is developed. The manufacturer and retailer will be required to abide by laws that are in place to protect the consumer. If the product is for a child, sharp or small parts that will come off when chewed or pulled, or long ribbons and cords, cannot be included as they might injure or choke the child. Children's nightwear must be labelled: 'Keep away from fire'. It is the designer's

Objectives

Understand the safety labelling symbols on textile products.

Have an awareness of safety testing and the standards that a product must meet in order to gain consumer confidence.

Appreciate consumer rights and responsibilities.

Consider the designer's role in consumer safety.

A *CE mark, Woolmark and Kitemark labels*

B *Fabric toys for children need to be designed with safety issues taken into consideration*

responsibility to ensure that appropriate fabrics, components and textile processes are used and that health and safety issues are taken into consideration.

New fabrics and fabric finishes might be selected by a designer to ensure that a product is safe and appealing to the consumer. Fabric that is **hypoallergenic** with **UV protection** may be chosen, such as that made from bamboo. Bamboo's organic and natural fibre properties make it non-irritating to the skin for anyone with skin sensitivities or allergies.

C *This toy is tested for flammability; the bear rapidly burns and hot melted material could injure a child and cause a widespread fire*

> **Remember**
>
> Designers should consider consumer rights when developing their design to ensure that it will meet required safety and quality standards.

> AQA **Examiner's tip**
>
> Be able to recognise quality, safety and warning symbols on product labels and explain why they are relevant to the specific target market.

> **Key terms**
>
> **Legislation:** laws.
>
> **Flammability:** liability to catch fire.
>
> **Hazard:** a step or process that could cause harm or injury.
>
> **Hypoallergenic:** unlikely to cause an allergic reaction.
>
> **UV protection:** will shield wearer from harmful ultra-violet radiation in sunlight.

D *Bamboo and wool sweater that is non-itchy*

> **Activity**
>
> Make a collection of 10 different labels found on home-furnishing and fashion products; check that it is safe to remove the labels, or copy down the details on small pieces of paper. You may need to search inside the garments or underneath the products. Look carefully at each label to understand what is written on it. Now see if you can match up the cut-out or copied labels with the original products.

⚭ **links**

Find out more at **www.tradingstandards.gov.uk** – information about trading standards and consumer rights.

www.bambooclothes.com – information about a new, safe and sustainable fabric.

See Labelling, pages 38–39, to learn more about labels.

See Fabric finishes, pages 30–31, for more information about fabric finishes.

> **Summary**
>
> There are regulations in place to protect consumer rights to ensure that textile products meet required standards.
>
> Certification trademarks and safety-guarantee symbols are used on labels to gain consumer confidence.
>
> Designers must consider health and safety issues when developing a new product.

kerboodle!

5.6 Health and safety: risk assessments

Keeping the textile workers safe

Health and safety at work is the responsibility of both employers and employees. Manufacturers are required by law to follow strict rules and regulations to make sure that the workers are protected from possible dangers when using machinery and handling materials. The workers must follow all safety rules and instructions to keep themselves and those around them safe.

Risk assessment

The dangers, hazards or risks involved in making a product can be identified, described and listed. This is known as risk assessment. In the workplace it is essential to know what might cause harm or injury to people or the environment, so that safety precautions and systems can be put in place to prevent accidents.

In the workplace a health and safety officer will:

- carry out risk assessments
- organise safety training, including first aid, for the workforce
- display warning notices, safety rules and fire exit signs
- ensure that machinery, equipment, tools and materials are stored safely, have safety guards and are safe for use, and are regularly tested for safety
- check that workers wear protective clothing, ear defenders, masks, safety gloves and footwear
- ensure that all processes are safe and will not damage the health of the employees
- ensure that chemicals used in manufacturing processes are recorded, stored and used safely, then recycled or disposed of safely
- check that the environment is safe with clean and tidy work areas and adequate ventilation to remove dust and fumes, and has noise-level control.

Safety measures include the proper training of machine operators, which is essential throughout the production line and across the workplace.

Objectives

Understand what is meant by risk assessment.

Appreciate the dangers at each stage in manufacture and the importance of safe working practices in a safe work environment.

A *Hazards during materials handling and sewing include injuries from fast running machines with sharp needles, inhalation of dust and back injuries from poor posture when seated*

⚭ links

Find out more at **www.hse.gov.uk** – see how health and safety in the textile industry is assessed and how risks can be controlled.

B *Risk assessment in garment manufacture*

Manufacturing stage	Hazards	Safety measures
Materials arrive in factory and are stored	Head injury from overhead transport system. Trapped fingers and feet from moving conveyors, trolleys and vehicles. Tripping over stacked materials, falling from steps and platforms	Hard hats worn. Danger areas marked with black-and-yellow warning strips, designated walkways. Safety guards and protective clothing, gloves and footwear worn
Fabric spread and pieces cut out using band saw	Finger and hand injuries from spreading machine and cutting blades. Dust inhalation	Use finger guard, protective chainmail gloves and steel toecap footwear
Fusing interlinings	Burns to fingers and hands from hot plates, feeding and unloading machines, inhalation of vapours	Use a press that is controlled by both hands, one person per machine. Ventilation to remove vapours

Sewing	Finger and hand injuries from needles and blades, eye injuries from broken needles, pulled hair from thread or fabric feed. High noise level may damage hearing. Seating may cause back injuries	Finger guards and eye shields/goggles used. Long hair tied up and no loose clothing. Seats adjusted for correct posture
Scissors, blades and needles	Cuts and pricks to fingers	All sharp blades, scissors and sharps (needles and pins) stored safely. Finger guards used
Pressing and steaming	Burns and scalds to fingers and hands from hot plates and steam, feeding and unloading machines, inhalation of vapours	Use a press that is controlled by both hands, one person per machine. Use a steam room rather than steaming individual garments. Ventilation to remove vapours
Cleaning and stain removal	Inhalation of solvent vapours, skin damage or reaction to contact with solvents. Fire hazard. Toxic chemicals	Ventilation to remove vapours. Solvent containers labelled with warnings. No sources of ignition
Production line handling	Head injury from overhead transport system. Trapped fingers and feet from moving conveyors, trolleys and vehicles. Tripping over stacked material	Hard hats worn. Danger areas marked with black-and-yellow warning strips, designated walkways. Safety guards and protective clothing, gloves and footwear worn
Packaging	Finger and hand injuries from cutting, folding and heat sealing during packaging	Ventilation to remove vapours from heat sealers. Safety guards and protective clothing, gloves and footwear worn

Safety can be increased by using automated machinery and computers to assist in materials handling, particularly where loads are heavy, or with fast-running machinery where heat, or sharp blades or needles are involved. Safety devices are used to check that machine settings are correct and to stop machinery in an emergency.

C *Automated chamber steam tunnels make this stage of manufacturing safer for employees*

Activity

1 During the manufacture of textile products there is a risk of contamination of the product with needles and pins. As a safety measure, machinists are only allowed one needle at a time. When a needle breaks, a supervisor will be called over to replace the broken needle. If the broken parts cannot be found, a metal detector is used to track down the broken pieces. A product contaminated with sharp metal pieces is unsafe for workers and a danger to future consumers and so cannot be left in the production line.

a Look around the classroom work area. What are the dangers involved in using the school sewing machines? Write a risk assessment listing the dangers and possible injuries or harm to students working on the machines.

b Design a safety notice for the classroom to tell students what to do when a needle breaks.

Remember

Production planning should include risk assessment and health and safety guidelines.

AQA Examiner's tip

Be able to detail possible hazards, safe working practices, protective guards, clothing and systems in place to protect workers.

Summary

Manufacturers are required by law to assess the risks involved in making a product.

Workers are required to follow safe working practices and all safety rules.

The working environment must be safe for employees and warning signs must be displayed.

AQA Examination-style questions

1   For this exemplar question the design brief is:

- fashion bags for teenagers
- theme of 'Jungle Life' to inspire design ideas
- to consider methods of fastening used for bags
- a design suitable for industrial production.

(a) Use a pencil to draw and label two different design ideas for your product. Marks will be given for quality of the ideas and the notes and sketches. *(2 x 4 marks)*

(b) Choose one of your design ideas for development. Analyse and explain how your choice of fastening(s) answers the design brief. *(6 marks)*

(c) Who is the target market for your bag?

Give detailed reasons to explain why the design idea you have chosen will appeal to your target market. *(4 marks)*

2   (a) Designers need to check that their design ideas will be successful. Describe three different ways of testing a new idea. *(6 marks)*

(b) (i) Designers usually make a final prototype of a new product. What is a prototype? *(2 marks)*

(b) (ii) Give three detailed reasons for making a prototype. *(6 marks)*

3   (a) What is the difference between standard cotton and organic cotton? *(2 marks)*

(b) What is meant by the 'recycling of textiles'? *(3 marks)*

(c) (i) What is meant by 'risk assessment'? *(2 marks)*

(ii) Give three possible dangers when using textile machinery and handling materials and for each of the three dangers explain how precautions can be put in place to prevent injury to workers. *(6 marks)*

(d) Many fashionable textile products are designed to have a short life span and are discarded when fashions change. Discuss the environmental issues related to the manufacture of such 'throw away' products? *(6 marks)*

AQA Examination-style questions

AQA Examiner's tip

- Be clear and detailed when explaining the advantages of carrying out research looking at existing products.

- Always give a full, detailed answer to gain maximum marks, especially when explaining the meaning of sustainability in textile product design.

- Give examples to further explain your answer, especially when discussing ethical issues.

- Be aware of new developments in technology and current social issues that may affect product design.

Processes and manufacture

To make successful textile products, the correct and most appropriate hand tools, equipment and machinery must be selected. In this section you will learn about methods of working, processes and systems and the use of computers in the textile industry. Illustrations show a wide range of textile machines, and there are suggested links to the internet to see more details and machines in action. Basic construction techniques are explained with notes and diagrams to help with sampling and making tasks, building on subject knowledge and understanding.

All designers work to develop their ideas, and this section tells you about modelling to test ideas, techniques and processes as an essential aspect of designing and making. You will need to know about production planning and how to build the documents used to record making details, such as the manufacturing specification and flowchart for the making and costing of a product. Chapter 7, Production planning, will help you with this aspect of processes and manufacture.

Computers are used at every stage in product design and manufacture and the final chapter of this section will explain how they benefit those working in the textile industry.

■ What will you study in this section?

After completing Processes and manufacture (Chapters 6–8) you should have a good understanding of:

- some of the different hand tools, equipment and machines used in textile production
- the production systems and their processes
- how to develop and modify products and ideas
- the basic construction techniques and methods
- the importance of production flowcharts
- how to put together a manufacturing specification and how they are used
- the different costs involved in making a product
- the use of quality control during production
- the use of ICT at all stages of research, design and manufacture.

■ Activities

For each of the chapter topics listed above, an exciting activity is suggested. The wide range of activities asks you to research, identify, collect, calculate, examine, draw, design, make a PowerPoint presentation, modify a pattern, write and make a transfer print. Some of the things to do can be presented to display in the classroom, to help others learn from your work. Other activities ask you to find things out or to design and make things, in order to help you learn more about processes and manufacture.

How will you use the information?

In Unit 1 (Written paper), you will be tested on your subject knowledge and understanding. An awareness of CAD and CAM is required and of industrial and commercial practice in textile product manufacturing. In Unit 2 (Controlled assessment), you will need to show that you can select and use appropriate manufacturing processes and techniques including CAD and CAM where appropriate. Also, your folder work and made piece will need to demonstrate your textile skills and subject knowledge of techniques and processes, production planning and computer technology.

6 Techniques and processes

6.1 Hand tools and equipment

It is important to select the correct tools and equipment, to know how to use them safely and effectively and to maintain them in clean, undamaged condition. This will allow the person using the tools and equipment to produce accurate work, resulting in a well-made product.

Objectives

Consider the range of basic hand tools used in making textile products.

Understand the purpose of each tool, and how to use them correctly, safely and effectively.

Activities

1 Identify and make a list of all the tools and equipment in your textiles classroom, under the following headings:

a Design

b Colouring and embellishing

c Measuring, marking

d Sharps

e Sewing

f Heating and pressing

g Computer.

2 Do you think the storage places and the layout of tools and equipment in your classroom are helpful to students? Write down three improvements that could be made.

Hand tools and equipment for designing, colouring and embellishing

The following tools and equipment are the basic kit required for designing, colouring and embellishing fabric:

- a range of pencils, pens, scissors and rulers
- colouring equipment to dye fabric, such as fabric crayons, fabric pens, fabric paint, print paste, powder or liquid dye
- protective apron and gloves to prevent dye from staining fingers and clothing
- brushes, **spray diffusers**, screens and **squeegees** to apply the dye or fabric-print paste
- a range of needles for hand stitching, decorative stitching and beading work (beading is done with long, very fine needles so that even the smallest

A *Equipment for colouring fabric*

group of beads can be threaded along the needle, whereas stitching through open-weave fabric with a woollen thread is done more easily using a blunt-ended needle with a large eye)

- a metal or wooden hoop for use in embroidery to keep the fabric flat when stitching; this improves accuracy and makes it safe when using a needle.

Hand tools and equipment for measuring and marking

- Flexible measuring tapes are used to measure curved surfaces accurately. A **pattern master** is used when making paper patterns to help draw curved lines and add seam allowance.
- Tailor's chalk or soft pencils are used to transfer markings on to fabric.

Hand tools and equipment for cutting

B *A designer cuts out pattern pieces using large scissors called shears*

- Craft knives allow for more detailed and accurate results than scissors, when cutting stencils for spray and print techniques. Use of mats when cutting with a knife prevents leaving cutting marks on the table surface.
- Scissors are made in a variety of sizes according to their purpose. Short, sharp scissors are useful for detailed cutting work when snipping threads during embroidery or clipping curves when pressing seams, whereas longer, thicker blades will cut across fabric quickly and more easily. **Pinking shears** help with edge finishing to neaten fabric. Left-handed people need scissors with blades aligned for them.
- Seam rippers will make the job of unpicking seams easier and quicker. There will be less chance of cutting the fabric instead of the stitching thread when using this hand tool.

Heated equipment

- Irons or heating presses are used to flatten fabric, press seams open, heat set fabric or heat transfer print designs on to fabric. Ironing or pressing is more effective if steam is also applied.

- Heated pots are used to melt the wax used in batik. Metal tainting tools, which look like a small metal bowl on a long handle, heat up to keep the wax warm and fluid, and are used to transfer the wax on to the fabric. The pot has a lid, a short cord and has a thermostatic control to ensure safety. This is important because if the wax overheats it could ignite; if it spills it could burn the person using the hot wax.

C *Sublimation printing transfers fabric ink printed on to paper on to polyester fabric*

Blocks and manikins

When developing, modelling, making and testing textile products it is helpful to use a frame to support a three-dimensional shape:

- Hat makers use a head-shaped block to enable them to mould felt to the correct shape.

- Fashion designers use a **manikin** to give correct figure measurements and body shape to build patterns from and to check garments for fit.

- Pins are used to hold fabric pieces in position on the manikin, and to temporarily join pieces, prior to tacking or stitching.

D *A designer using a manikin to test a calico fabric prototype*

Computers

Using computers, software packages and equipment linked to them, such as digital cameras and printers, will speed up the creative process, offer greater accuracy and broaden the range of textile techniques available to aid designing, manufacture and presentation.

Summary

Appropriate tools and equipment should be selected, used correctly and safely, and stored in the designated place.

A wide variety of tools and equipment are required when designing and making.

Efficient and accurate use of tools and equipment will help to ensure that high-quality products are made.

∞ links

See Dyeing and printing, pages 40–41, for more information about batik.

See Health and safety: risk assessment, pages 88–89, for more information about safe use of tools and equipment.

See Chapter 8, ICT, for more details about the use of computers.

Remember

- Check tools are clean and sharp before use.
- Check health and safety rules before using tools and sharps.
- Organise tools and store in a safe place.

AQA Examiner's tip

Be able to recognise and name each measuring, marking and cutting tool and to list equipment required for each stage of making.

Key terms

Manikin: also mannequin; a dressmakers' dummy in a human-shaped form, for designing and testing garments.

6.2 Using machines in textile production

Industrial machinery

A very wide range of textile machinery is used to process fibres, spin yarn, construct fabric using knit, weave and bonding techniques, print, dye and finish it, and then make textile products from the fabric. Machinery speeds up each stage of manufacture, and makes some processes **automatic**. As long as the operators are well trained, machines can improve safety in the workplace, be more cost effective and make quality consistent. Machines to transport materials, monitor and inspect production and package finished products assist the workforce and speed production. Computerised machines have been introduced at most stages of production to simplify the route from design to manufacture and improve systems and control.

Objectives

Consider the variety of machines used in textile processes.

Appreciate the difference between sewing and embroidery machines.

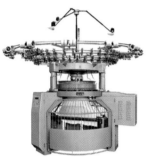
Cylinder knitting machine

Multi-head embroidery

Band saw

Embroidery machine

Digital jet printer

Overlocker

 A Some of the main types of machines used in the manufacture of textile products

Remember

Machinery can be operated by hand, be semi-automatic or fully automatic and can also be computer controlled.

Stitching by machine

There are many different types of sewing machine; some perform very specialist tasks such as making buttonholes, **overlocking** fabric edges or embroidering motifs.

Generally, a basic sewing machine can be used to join fabric pieces together and to decorate them with a small range of embroidery stitches. To operate the machine skilfully, training is essential and practice is required.

Diagram **B** shows the main parts of the sewing machine. Neat and accurate work is produced when the right type of needle is used and machine settings are appropriate for type of fabric stitched. For example, a ball-point needle and stretch stitch are required to join

Key terms

Automatic: operation carried out by machine, to assist an operator (semi-automatic) or to complete the task independently (fully automatic).

Overlocking: a method of neatening seams in industry using a machine with three or more threads to trim, stitch and edge-finish the seam.

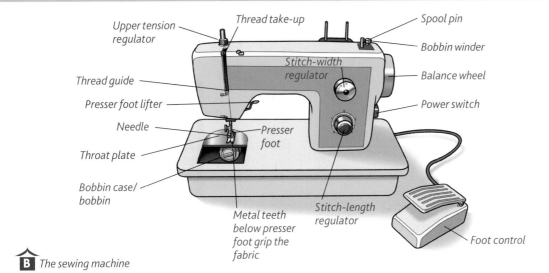

Upper tension regulator
Thread take-up
Spool pin
Bobbin winder
Stitch-width regulator
Balance wheel
Thread guide
Power switch
Presser foot lifter
Needle
Presser foot
Throat plate
Bobbin case/ bobbin
Metal teeth below presser foot grip the fabric
Stitch-length regulator
Foot control

B The sewing machine

knitted fabric, to ensure that the fabric is not damaged while stitching and that the seam made is as stretchy as the knitted fabric.

Computerised embroidery machines are used to interpret digitised artwork so that original designs can be scanned, outlined and filled with decorative stitching and then reproduced on to fabric as embroidery. The machine can also embroider from a design menu to stitch patterns, panels, motifs and to personalise products with written script and numbers.

The operator prepares the fabric to be embroidered, by ironing a light interfacing onto the back of the fabric to stabilise it. The fabric is held in a frame to present a flat surface for stitching. A range of different threads can be selected to colour the embroidery.

∞ links

See Health and safety: risk assessments, pages 88–89.
See Quality control, pages 118–119.

AQA *Examiner's tip*

Be familiar with the sewing machine and learn how to spot and correct sewing faults such as puckering of fabric and uneven or missed stitching.

Indigo Clothing

Indigo Clothing uses machines to print and embroider T-shirts, which are customised for each order. The company is keen to ensure that the product meets the client's expectations; it explains on its website that 'Some people want cheap, disposable, promotional T-shirts where a rock-bottom price is key, whilst others need a high-quality, fashion item which best reflects their brand'.

How many different qualities of T-shirt are offered by Indigo Clothing? What recommendations are made by the company when the client is deciding between screen printing and transfer printing for their T-shirt order?

www.indigoclothing.com

Case study

Summary

Machines speed up the process of making and can be used to ensure high-quality products.

Many machines have fast-moving parts and sharp needles. Great care must be taken to follow safety rules to avoid injury while operating such a machine.

Production systems and processes

Production systems

There are three main types of production **system**:

- one-off
- batch
- mass.

When planning which production system to use, a manufacturer will need to consider the product type know how many products are to be made and the timing of delivery dates. Choice of system will affect the way fabrics and components are ordered and what sort of training the workforce will need. Large-scale production reduces the cost of manufacturing each product. Factory floor layout of **workstations** and production lines will be determined by the type of system in place.

Activity

Look in magazines and cut out pictures to make a collection of designer outfits from catwalk shows. Why are these garments made by one-off production? How much do the clothes and accessories cost to buy? What type of person would want these exclusive products?

One-off

Individual items are made once, by hand or by highly skilled machine operators. One-off products are exclusive and made by a craftsperson or designer-maker to meet an individual client's requirements. This production system is also known as bespoke, made-to-measure, custom-made or jobbing production. **Haute couture** garments are made in this way.

Batch

A team of workers will work to complete an agreed number of identical products. Production costs are lower than for one-off products.

Mass

Large numbers of identical products are manufactured over a long period of time. This is also known as volume production and usually involves a production line to make items that are in continual demand such as white T-shirts. It is the cheapest system because materials can be bought in bulk and automated machinery and computer-aided manufacture is used as much as possible to cut labour costs.

Production lines

In mass production each machine operator works on a section of the product before passing it along to the next machinist to carry out the next stage of making. The workers must ensure that they work speedily to agreed standards so that the whole production line runs smoothly and is very cost effective. For cheap, simple products the machinery often runs continuously with machine operators working shifts.

Objectives

Understand what is meant by one-off, batch and mass production.

Learn about line production and subassembly systems.

Consider the cost implications when selecting a method of production.

A *Matthew Williamson designs dresses for red carpet events for celebrities such as Sienna Miller, Jade Jagger, Nicole Kidman and Kylie Minogue*

B *A Per Una dress: Marks & Spencer orders a batch of print dresses in sizes 8–20 to stock its major stores with a product that will feature as a short-term item in its range of summer dresses*

Subassembly

It may be more efficient to join and attach small parts of a product together in an operation separate from the main production line. For example, a whole shirt collar is made before attaching it to the top of the shirt. Some production systems may have several subassemblies, some of which may be done in another workplace.

Just-in-time stock control (JIT)

This is a cost-effective method of ordering fabrics, components and sub-assemblies to arrive just before they are needed. Stock storage time is reduced but any mistakes and delays in deliveries will hold production up.

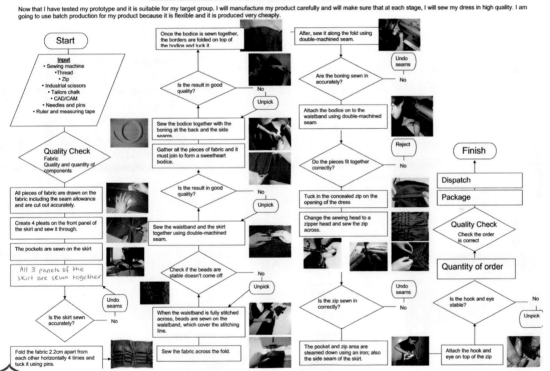

C *Jenny decides to use batch production to make her dress; she presents the information using a flowchart with photos and written notes*

Summary

Hand-crafted, exclusive products are made individually using the one-off production system.

For a fixed number of identical products, batch production is cost effective.

Mass production usually includes production lines.

Subassemblies are made separately before they are joined to the main product.

Key terms

System: the method of putting together the individual parts.

Workstations: areas laid out to enable the worker to organise resources, use correct machinery and stack completed work in the most efficient way.

Haute couture: the French term for the highest quality designer garments.

▊ Modelling to test ideas, techniques and processes

3D modelling

Many ideas start on paper as simple sketches by hand or on the computer. It is also a good idea to work in a three-dimensional way to explore possible ideas for trying out shaping the product and creating design features; this is called modelling.

Some designers choose to model in paper; a paper model is inexpensive and can easily be cut to size and manipulated. Garment designers use a manikin when testing the model; they also drape and pin lengths of fabric around it to see what might work. Digital photos can be taken to record ideas, and then the photos can be sketched over to further develop ideas.

Activity

Select a simple commercial pattern for a basic fashion top or dress that is easy and quick to use. Cut around each pattern piece and lay each one out; make sure they are lightly pressed to iron out creases.

Now decide whether you will lengthen or shorten the garment. Find the pattern alteration line; this will normally be about two-thirds down the length of the pattern piece. Now pleat the paper pattern along this line to reduce the length and shorten the garment, or cut across the line and insert extra paper to lengthen. See Diagram **B**.

How do you think this would be done in industry?

Remember

The purpose of sampling and modelling is to test ideas during product development and to communicate ideas about the design to the client.

CAD

Here is a 2D image of my final dress using paint on my computer. This shows a detail image of how my dress will look like.

FRONT VIEW   BACK VIEW

Using CAD (computer aided design) is very useful because it allows changes to be made quickly so I can experiment other colours and improvements in the development of the dress.

It can save money as CAD shows a visualized image of the product so you won't need to make prototypes. Also, it is easier to produce the dress better and the development of the dress.

A *Jenny uses newspaper to model her dress idea and the computer to develop her dress design*

Pattern development

An existing pattern, such as a commercial pattern or block pattern, can be altered by hand to make it fit new design ideas and then a **toile** can be made up from the modified pattern. A pattern can also be made through disassembly of an existing product.

The designer uses a pattern that is similar to the new design to be made up. Separate pattern pieces can then be lengthened or shortened, given more fullness or made more tight fitting or the shape slightly changed. If one pattern piece is changed then other connecting pieces may have to be altered too. This may be done to raise a waistline, shorten a sleeve or enlarge an armhole, etc.

Key terms

Toile: a model of a garment often made from inexpensive cotton calico.

⚭**links**

See Product disassembly, pages 62–63 to find out more about pattern development.

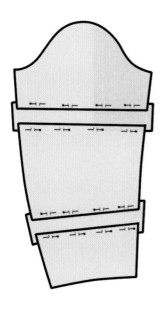 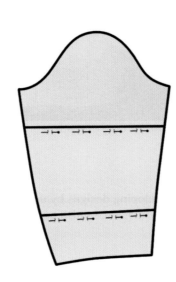

A *To lengthen, cut straight across the pattern piece at the two positions indicated and insert two strips of paper to fill the gaps*

B *To shorten, fold and pin tucks in pattern paper at the two positions indicated*

B *How to lengthen and shorten a sleeve pattern pieces*

From the new pattern further developments can be made to extend the range of products in a collection. For example, within the collection there might be a blouse, a short dress and a longer dress, all with the same neckline design.

Moulage

Fashion designers may decide to make their own pattern by modelling with calico fabric on a manikin; this is known as moulage. The manikin is taped to show where seams will be, then the sections are traced and a paper pattern is made. A toile from the new pattern can then be stitched together.

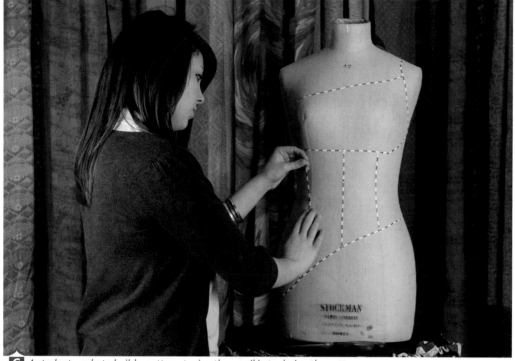

C *A student works to build a pattern, taping the manikin to design the pattern*

Using computers

Most designers will speed the process of developing designs by using computer software to draw and fill in colour. Images can also be imported, or scanned, and quickly edited.

D *A designer uses a computer to keep a library of ideas which are suitable for development*

Pattern generation software is used by designers to build new patterns from standard designs, which can then be printed out. The software can also be used to develop the pattern into a range of different sizes, for example from size 8 to size 22. This is called pattern grading.

In industry when designers have to work through development rapidly, working closely with clients, design activities can be linked through to making prototypes and then the final batch of products. Often new product ideas are based on updating last season's best-selling lines, or interpreting predicted fashion trends.

Purpose of sampling and prototypes

It is sometimes unnecessary to make up the whole product, when smaller samples can be made to investigate and test techniques and present ideas to clients. A designer might store such samples in reference files, using them as starting points to build a new product.

Designers make samples, toiles or prototypes to test techniques and method of making and to look at costing implications. Often a supplier will work with a designer to modify fabric or component design for the new product being developed.

Models try on prototype garments so that the designer can make further adjustments to the pattern to ensure that the fit is correct. When the final design is agreed and a product specification written, a set of standards in a range of product sizes can be made, using full production techniques and processes.

links

See Use of ICT in manufacturing, pages 126–127, for more details.

AQA *Examiner's tip*

- Be able to describe ways of trying out colourways, ideas about shape, style and use of different fabric.
- Be clear about the reasons for testing techniques and processes.

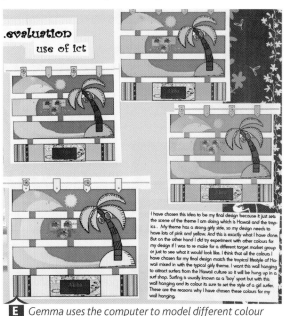

E *Gemma uses the computer to model different colour options for her wall hanging design*

Summary

Modelling and sampling will help the designer test ideas to develop the product.

New designs can be developed from existing products.

Computers can speed up development work.

Learning basic construction techniques

It is a good idea to use simple commercial patterns to make up a variety of garments in order to gain experience and learn sewing techniques. Pattern instructions give clear, step-by-step written notes and diagrams to show how to join pieces together, finish seams, hem and follow simple construction techniques.

To see how basic construction techniques are done, you can look on the internet to find video clips and simple instructions for a wide range of sewing skills. The following basic techniques are useful to know.

Objectives

Understand how to join fabric and finish fabric edges.

Consider how fabric can be manipulated to control volume and shape the product.

Making seams

Flat seam

This is the most commonly used seam. It is pressed open and flat, and is usually neatened using any of the techniques described in the next section. If the fabric is knitted a stretch stitch is used that will allow the stitched seam to stretch as much as the fabric needs to in use.

Activities

1. Using a digital camera and computer, make a simple PowerPoint presentation to show how to make a flat seam. How many slides will you need to include each stage of making?

2. Show the presentation to your class and ask them to make up a sample following your instructions. How could you improve your step-by-step method?

A flat seam is the basic seam joining the edges of two pieces of fabric. It is used on normal-weight fabrics where there is no special strain on the seam. In most cases, plain straight stitch is used to stitch the seam.

1 With the right side a of the fabric facing, pin the fabric together at both ends of the seam line and at intervals along the seam line, leaving an allowance of 2 cm.

2 Tack close to the seam line and remove pins. Then stitch along the seam line, backstitching a couple of stitches at each end to secure.

3 After removing the tacking stitches finish the seam edge by pinking it or as necessary for the fabric.

4 Press the seam as stitched and then press it open as shown, using a pressing cloth between the iron and the fabric.

 Making a flat seam

French seam

The French seam is particularly useful when a fabric is delicate and prone to fraying, such as chiffon. Raw edges are concealed inside a double-stitched seam.

This is a narrow seam.

A French seam is generally used for fine fabrics or for those which fray easily. It is a seam within a seam and when finished should be about 5 mm or less in width.

1 *Trimmed seam allowance.*

Place the wrong sides of the fabric together. Pin and tack in position close to the seam line. Stitch 5 mm to the right of the seam. Press as stitched. Then trim the seam allowance to 3 mm.

2 *Fabric pinned in place.*

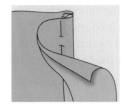

Press the seam open. Then turn the right sides of the fabric together. Fold on the stitch line and press. Tack in position.

3 *Finished French seam.*

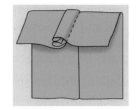

Stitch along the seam line and press as stitched.

B *Making a French seam*

Flat fell seam

This gives strength and decoration to a product. Denim jeans are made strong by this technique. A double line of stitching is often used in a contrasting coloured thread.

This is a heavy-duty seam, providing a neat finish for either side of the fabric.

A flat fell seam is a very strong neat seam which withstands heavy wear and frequent washing. You can choose which side of the seam you use on the right side of the fabric.

1 *Trimmed underseam.*

With the wrong sides of the fabric together, pin and tack along the seam line and press the seam open. Then press both seam edges over to one side. Trim the underseam allowance to half its width.

2 *Upper seam pinned in place.*

Turn the upper seam allowance edge evenly over the trimmed edge and pin into place.

3 *Top stitching.*

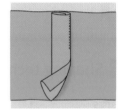

Top stitch along the turned-over edge, removing the pins, and press as stitched.

C *Making a flat fell seam*

Neatening seams

Pinking

Pinking shears are used to cut a zigzag edge along a woven fabric edge. This helps to prevent the woven threads from unravelling, as seen in Diagram **A** (making a flat seam).

Overlocking and zigzag stitching

An overlocker with three or more threads is used simultaneously to trim, stitch and neaten the seam. Photo **D** shows the chain of stitches made by the overlocker overcasts the fabric edge to keep it from unravelling. This is an inexpensive way to neaten the seam.

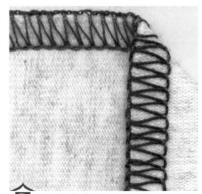

D *Overlocked seam*

Bias binding

When it is essential to cover the fabric edge, **bias binding** can be folded in half and stitched along both edges of the flat seam. Seams in more expensive fashion clothing often feature bound edges. This technique can also be a cheaper alternative to making a fully lined garment.

In clothing that has special high-performance features, the seams are taped, for example in a wetsuit. The water movement through the seam is restricted by the tape and the seams are also strengthened.

E *This ski jacket features taped seams to make the jacket more weatherproof*

Shaping techniques

Darts

Darts are used to create 3D shaping in flat fabric in order to fit the figure. A dart in the fabric is useful at the waist or bust where a pointed fold is made to shape the garment panel. Darts are stitched along the fold line and pressed down, towards the side seam.

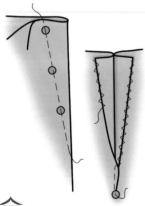

1 *Fold dart, right sides together matching small perforations and stitch tapering to a point at single perforation. Press dart to one side.*

2 *If using a heavy material, cut dart at fold and press it open. Oversew the edges to neaten.*

F *Making a dart*

Pleating

A pleat is a fold in the fabric, which can be pressed in order to keep its edge or stitched down along a section of the fold. Skirts are often pleated to allow for ease of movement at the knee. On some shirt-front panels, very small pleats called pin tucks are stitched down to give a decorative effect.

Alexander McQueen

Tartan fabric and the influence of traditional Scottish kilts are seen in this fashion collection. Pleats and gathers are used to drape the fabric asymmetrically around the figure. Look at the whole collection on the internet. How many different ways are these techniques used to shape the garments and create volume in the styles?

See www.style.com to view Alexander McQueen Autumn/Winter 2006 collection.

G *Traditional kilt pleating inspires Alexander McQueen in his Autumn/ Winter 2006 collection*

Gathering

Fabric width can be reduced by gathering to give a wavy shaping to curtains or garment waistlines or sleeves. Fabric volume is controlled by two lines of long stitches at the top edge of the fabric. The two threads on one side of the fabric are gently pulled taut as the fabric is eased back along the length of the threads. This technique is useful when inserting sleeves; the sleeve top is gathered and the fullness distributed according to the fit around the armhole opening, with the majority of the gathering around the shoulder.

To ease in fullness at top of sleeve, make a row of machine stitching along seam line and 6 mm INSIDE seam line between notches, using a long machine-stitch

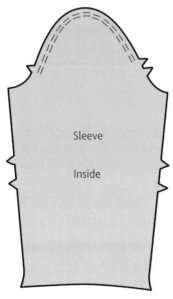

Sleeve

Inside

Inserting a sleeve

∞ links

Find out more at
www.isew.co.uk – get clear and helpful information about sewing techniques and handy hints to solve sewing problems.

www.youtube.com – see sewing techniques demonstrated on video.
www.bbc.co.uk/schools/ gcsebitesize/design/textiles/ productiontechniques – has helpful notes about techniques and processes.

Remember

Select the correct technique, according to fabric type and weight.

AQA Examiner's tip

Be able to draw simple diagrams to show techniques to make seams, finish fabric edges and manipulate fabric by gathering, pleating or making darts.

Key terms

Bias binding: a fabric strip cut diagonally across fabric. The long edges are folded under and the strip is folded in half along its length. This is the binding strip that can be used to cover the raw edge of other fabrics.

Summary

Fabric is joined using seams that are appropriate for the fabric used.

Seams are neatened according to the type of fabric and target market requirements.

Fabric volume can be manipulated to add shape, style and surface decoration to a product.

Methods for making

There is often a choice of method to use when constructing features such as pockets, tabs, collars, cuffs and **plackets,** or when inserting zips or adding a **facing**. The designer will need to consider fabric type and weight and whether the construction technique is also to be decorative. **Interlining** may need to be fused to the back of the fabric to strengthen it when constructing collars, plackets, pocket openings and flaps.

More complex procedures will take longer to make and the machinists will need more skill. Linings and interlinings will add to the cost, as will larger features that need extra fabric (e.g. gathers or pleats) or complex fastenings.

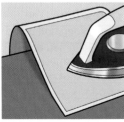

A   *Parts of a shirt*

Compare the different types of pockets in Source **B**. The pockets are a special design feature of this uniform and each has a particular purpose. Look carefully at the use of hook-and-loop (Velcro) fastening used to secure the pocket openings.

Product analysis and disassembly can be carried out to find out how a constructed feature could be made or a fastening added to the product.

How to make a simple patch pocket

A patch pocket is made from one piece of fabric folded in two and stitched onto the garment. It can have square or rounded edges at the base.

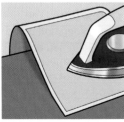

1 *Iron the fusible interfacing to the wrong side of the outer pocket. Fold the pocket over so the right sides are together and pin into place. Stitch the pocket, leaving an opening for turning it right side out in the centre of the bottom edge. Backstitch ends of stitching.*

Objectives

Understand some basic construction techniques.

Consider how product costing is increased by additional stages in product manufacture.

⚭ links

Find out more at **www.isew.co.uk** get clear and helpful information about sewing techniques and handy hints to solve sewing problems.
See Fastenings, pages 46–47 to learn about different types of fastenings.

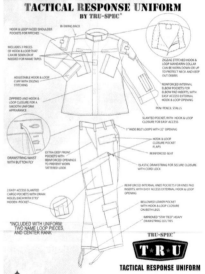

B *Pockets feature on the Tru-spec Tactical Response uniform*

⚭ links

See Product disassembly, pages 58–59.

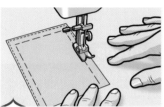

2 *Trim the corners or, if the corners are rounded, notch into the seam allowance at the curve. Pull the pocket through the opening, turning right side out and press.*

3 *Pin and tack the pocket on to the garment. Start to stitch (1 cm) from the top right hand corner and backstitch just into garment fabric to reinforce. Stitch close to pocket edge on three sides, finishing securely.*

C *How to make a simple patch pocket*

Stitching a zip in place

Prepare and stitch the seam, leaving an opening for the zip the length of the zip teeth (see 1). Press the seam allowance open Neaten the edges of the seam allowances using the appropriate method. Pin and tack along the fold lines (see 2). Pin the zip into

position with the teeth centred over the seam (see 3). Tack (6 mm) from zip teeth then remove pins. Stitch close to the tacking on the right side using the zip foot. Start at the top, stitch down the length of one side (see. 4). Remove the tacking and press.

1 *Aligning the zip*   **2** *Tacking fold lines*   **3** *Pinning the zip*   **4** *Sewing the zip*

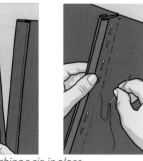  

D *Stitching a zip in place*

Making buttonholes

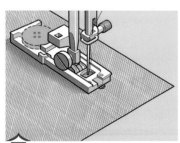 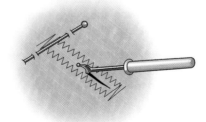

E *Making buttonholes*

A special automatic buttonholing foot is needed for the sewing machine. The sewing machine instruction book will describe how to make the buttonhole using the foot.

When cutting open the buttonhole, use a pin and a seam ripper to give an accurate result.

Key terms

Placket: the strip down the front opening of a shirt in which the buttonholes are stitched.

Facing: fabric is cut to the same pattern as the main fabric. The facing and main fabrics are placed right sides together, stitched around leaving a gap in the stitching, and then turned through. This results in a neat finished edge. For example, facing is used for sleeveless dress bodices.

Interlining: light bonded fabric that often has dry glue on one side. It can be ironed on to the reverse side of the main fabric to strengthen it. When the dry glue is heated it bonds the two layers together.

Summary

Construction techniques can be learnt through experience of following commercial patterns.

Some construction techniques are also decorative.

7.1 Production flowcharts

Planning for manufacture

In industry clear instructions need to be given to all the employees to enable them to work together efficiently. Production planning is required to ensure that:

- **resources** are organised
- stages of making are detailed
- order of making is logical
- quality of made pieces is monitored
- work schedules are met.

System for making

To make a product successfully a system is required, particularly when more than one product is to be made. A system consists of inputs, which are processed into outputs. For example, the input could be fabric and components; the process comprises the making stages; and the output is a batch of cushion covers.

The flowchart is used to show the system in diagram form. The start and finish points are recorded in a lozenge shaped box, the stages of making are shown in rectangular boxes. Arrows link the series of steps in manufacture.

Sub-assembly

During manufacture it is often necessary to attach small components when embellishing individual sections or to join smaller parts together before working on the main garment. This is called sub-assembly. It may even be carried out in a different workplace from the main place of manufacture, for example by skilled craft workers who add beads by hand or by another company that use specialist embroidery machinery.

Sub-assembly stages feed into the final assembly during which the main parts of the product are put together. The flowchart for the skirt in Diagram A includes a sub-assembly to make the skirt lining. The lining is made separately from the main skirt, and then the two parts are joined together at the waistband.

Flowchart feedback loops

It is important to monitor production to see if the made pieces meet the required standard at each stage of making. The manufacturing system needs to include **quality control (QC)** check points and these can be written into the flowchart.

Key terms

Resources: materials, people and machinery involved in making the product.

Quality control (QC): products are checked to assess whether they conform to set standards.

Remember

Do not forget to include quality control (QC) checks as part of the flowchart.

⃝⃝ links

See Quality assurance, pages 66–67, and Quality control, pages 118–69.

⃝⃝ links

Find out more at www.alibaba.com/company/10097938.html

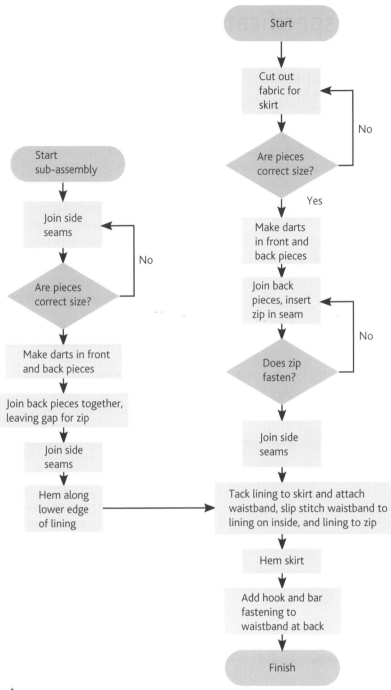

Start

↓

Cut out fabric for skirt

←── No

↓

Are pieces correct size?

Yes ↓

Make darts in front and back pieces

↓

Join back pieces, insert zip in seam

←── No

↓

Does zip fasten?

↓

Join side seams

↓

Tack lining to skirt and attach waistband, slip stitch waistband to lining on inside, and lining to zip

↓

Hem skirt

↓

Add hook and bar fastening to waistband at back

↓

Finish

Start sub-assembly

↓

Join side seams

←── No

↓

Are pieces correct size?

↓

Make darts in front and back pieces

↓

Join back pieces together, leaving gap for zip

↓

Join side seams

↓

Hem along lower edge of lining

A *Flowchart showing how to make a lined skirt*

B *A quality control check is made to see if the zip works properly*

Activity

Production planning flowchart poster design

Make a poster for the classroom to show how to make an appliquéd cushion cover with a buttonhole fastening on the back.

You will need to use flowchart boxes in the appropriate shapes and arrows to link the system.

How could you include sub-assemblies in the flowchart? Which quality control checks will you include?

Summary

A flowchart is a universal system used to plan work for the manufacture of a product.

A flowchart lists and puts into order the operations to be carried out during the manufacture of a product.

Symbols are used in the flowchart in order to simplify instructions.

When a check is made, if the work has been carried out correctly, the section can be passed on to the next stage of making. However, if standards are not met, the stage of making will have to be done again properly.

The flowchart in Diagram **A** shows the check points written inside diamond-shaped boxes, to show a decision is to be made. For example, the 'No' feedback loop will provide the instruction to repeat a stage of making to ensure that the zip does actually fasten correctly.

What to include in a manufacturing specification

The manufacturing specification describes the stages of manufacture and materials needed in order to make the product, using flowcharts, diagrams, notes and samples. If the product is to be made repeatedly, using a manufacturing specification will ensure that each product is identical and made to a set standard. Each manufacturer will have their own style of specification, developed to suit their particular system of working. It generally includes the following:

- product name, description, reference number and date
- **working drawing** or photo of product
- fabric and component details and samples
- specific tools needed, such as particular sewing machine needles
- pattern lay plan
- instructions for making
- quality control check points
- tolerance levels
- packaging requirements.

This is similar to a product specification for a final design; however, the manufacturing specification will also detail how the product is to be manufactured.

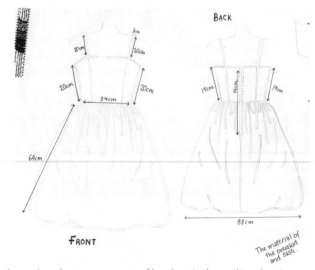

A Temitayo gives the measurements of her dress in the working drawing

Tolerance levels

Tolerance levels are given to ensure that when products are made in quantity they conform to a specified range of variance allowed on each process. Tolerance levels might be given for size of a product, seam allowance or for the placement of decorative motifs, pockets, buttons, etc. For example, in a batch of 45 x 45 cm cushion covers, the actual size may be permitted to vary between 44.5 cm and 45.5 cm each side; this is a tolerance level of 1 cm.

links

Find out more at **www.ripcurl.eu** – look at product design for surf and mountain wear.

See Fabric choice and specification, pages 34–37.

See Evaluating design specifications, pages 64–65.

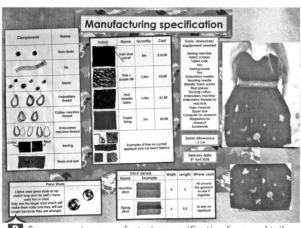
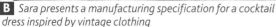

B Sara presents a manufacturing specification for a cocktail dress inspired by vintage clothing

C Ghetto Love Pants

Case study

RipCurl promotional product specification

A specification that details the features of a product is often used in promotional sales literature and online to advertise the special features of a product. The RipCurl 'Ghetto Love Pants' in Photo C are targeted at those who want quality skiwear that is also very fashionable. A tracking device is concealed within the trousers to enable a lost or injured skier to be located, and special construction techniques are used to make a very functional sports garment. Why do you think they are called 'Ghetto Love Pants'?

RipCurl Ghetto Love Pants

Colours

All-over print as shown

Material:

Two-layer Gore-Tex fabric with custom sublimation Ghetto Love all-over print

Construction

Regular fit, fully seam-taped, STL stitchless technology, 40 grs insulation

Features

Recco avalanche rescue system integrated
STL laser-cut pockets
Adjustable waistband
Alcatraz closure system
Waistband D-ring
Jacket–pant connector loops
Mesh-backed ventilation
Leg gaiter with boot hook
Kick patch

Activities

1 Read the specification for RipCurl Ghetto Love Pants in the case study. Draw some ideas for a coordinating ski jacket, designing a fashionable and useful garment with special features similar to the trousers. You may wish to visit the RipCurl website to get inspiration.

2 Now write a specification for your jacket design and present a working drawing to show back, front and close-up detail of design features.

Summary

The manufacturing specification provides all the detailed information required to make the product.

Tolerance levels are specified on a manufacturing specification to ensure that products are made to a consistent standard during batch or mass production.

Working drawings explain exactly what the product looks like from different viewpoints.

Costing a product

Product costing

A **spreadsheet** is used to list the costs involved in making a product. Direct costs include the cost of fabrics, components and the labour required to make the individual product. The **indirect costs** are shared out between all the products made and include costs of:

- research
- design and development
- machinery and equipment
- factory **overheads**
- cost of storage of stock materials
- staff training
- testing and quality control checks
- packaging
- transport
- advertising and marketing
- manufacturing profit.

When a product is made in a large batch or is mass produced, materials can be ordered in bulk and the costs of manufacturing and the overheads can be divided up between a greater number of products, to make each one less costly to produce.

The selling price of each product will need to include profit for the retailer. Student exemplar **A** shows a simple breakdown of costs. It is important to check the budget described in the design specification, to ensure that the final selling price is appropriate for the target market so that the product will sell.

If the final design is too costly to make, then modifications will need to be made. Choice of materials and the techniques used will need to be altered to reduce the costs but without affecting the quality or

Key terms

Spreadsheet: a table of data, which can be used to store information. Use Microsoft Excel to create spreadsheets and calculate data.

Indirect costs: business expenses not directly attributable to any particular product, also known as overheads.

Overheads: factory running costs – electricity for machinery, heating, lighting, water rates, building rent, administration costs, etc.

Comparative shop: research activity to compare and contrast two or more similar existing products; results may be presented as a report or in a table.

AQA Examiner's tip

Include indirect costs when working out the final cost of the product and consider the required profit when establishing the selling price.

Materials and components	Quantity	Unit cost (£)	Supplier	Total cost (£)
Blue velvet	3m	5.00	Bridlington Boyes	15.00
Pink + purple silk	1/4m	12.00	Fabric shop in Slovenia	3.00
Red metallic fabric	1/2m	3.00	Bridlington fabric shop	1.50
Purple lining	2m	2.50	Bridlington fabric shop	5.00
Navy cotton	1 reel	0.87	Bridlington Boyes	0.87
Purple cotton	1 reel	0.87	Bridlington Boyes	0.87
Navy zip	1	1.80	Bridlington Boyes	1.80
Multi-coloured beads	1 packet	3.00	Bridlington Boyes	3.00
Multi-coloured embroidery threads	1 packet	4.50	The sewing shop	4.50
Metal studs	1 packet	0.50	The sewing shop	0.50
Hook and eye	1 pair	0.20	The sewing shop	0.20
Fabric paints	1 set	2.00	Bridlington Boyes	2.00
Appliqué and cut-back fabrics	-	0	Re-cycled	0

Costing
Total direct cost (TDC) = £38.24
Overheads 15% of TDC = £11.47
Manufacturing cost = £49.71
Profit margin = 300% of manufacturing cost = £149.13
Selling price = profit margin + manufacturing cost = £198

A *Sara costs her cocktail dress and estimates the selling price*

appearance. Production efficiency is essential to limit materials wastage and keep to deadlines. If the time it takes to make each product is reduced, the cost will also be less for each product.

Product cost comparison

Designers often carry out a **comparative shop** to examine existing products during research. The cost of two or more products will be analysed as part of this.

The two dresses in Source **B** are similar to look at but the high street version is less expensive to buy than the designer dress. The Jill Stuart dress has a button-through front, elasticated smock detail, detachable spaghetti straps, a full skirt and is fully lined. The Topshop cherry print corset dress with exposed zip at the back is made from 97 per cent cotton, 3 per cent Elastane. The costs are higher for the Jill Stuart dress because the fabric includes silk, the fastening is more complex, it is lined and fewer dresses of that design have been made. In contrast, a large batch of the machine-washable Topshop dress has been produced for a nationwide chain of stores. The costs are not the same for the two dresses and this is reflected in the difference in selling price.

B Two different versions of a cherry print dress

Ethical issues

Costs can be reduced by manufacturing the product in developing countries, where wages and factory costs and overheads are generally much lower than in the UK. However, some of these manufacturers may not have health and safety regulations in place or policies to prevent pollutants from being released into the environment; wages may be unfair or children might be employed. It is important to consider these issues and also the costs of transport. Some consumers are willing to pay more for fairtrade or local products.

Activity

A designer needs 1.5 m of fabric to make a skirt, plus a zip, thread, decorative beads, one button, 1 m lining fabric and 0.25 m of interfacing. Make two different spreadsheets to detail the cost of making the skirt, using (1) silk fabric at £12.00 per m and (2) polyester satin fabric at £4.00 per m. You could check the cost of the components in a shop, catalogue or on the internet.

What is the difference in cost between the silk and the polyester skirt?

Remember

There are many aspects involved in costing a product and determining its selling price.

⬭links

See Production systems and processes, pages 100–101, for more details about methods of production. See Moral issues, pages 76–77, and Environmental issues and sustainability, pages 82–83, for more on moral, ethical and environmental issues.

Summary

Ethical issues influence the costing of products.

Costs of designing and making a product are reduced if the product is to be mass produced; here are economies of scale.

A prototype product is often modified to reduce costs, prior to full-scale production.

7.4 Quality control

■ Critical control points

In Quality assurance, pages 66–7 it was explained how quality assurance is planned into the design of a product. This section concerns specific quality control (QC) checks made during the manufacturing stages as part of the production flowchart. These quality control checks ensure that raw materials are fit for use, products are produced according to specifications and the final product is safe and conforms to prescribed standards.

Quality control checks take place at three main **critical control points** (CCPs) during the manufacture of a product. These checks are made on the raw materials, the prototype and on samples taken from the production run.

1 Raw materials check

Objectives

Consider how quality can be tested and monitored during production.

Understand that there are three main critical control points during the manufacture of a product.

AQA **Examiner's tip**

Be able to explain some critical control points in product manufacture.

Key terms

Critical control points (CCPs): the stages at which checks are made.

A *Fabric rolls are examined to check condition*

Raw materials are checked to make sure they are in good condition, the correct order has been delivered from the supplier, and the fabric specification has been met. Fabric should be clean and of the correct type, width, colour, weight and fibre content. Components are similarly checked; fastenings should fit together securely.

2 Prototype testing

The sample maker considers the design and making details of the product as they make a prototype. They trial the design and try to troubleshoot any potential cutting and sewing problems that could arise in production and pass that information back to the production manager. The prototype is tested against the design specification to see how successful the fabrics and components are and whether the product is safe and fit for purpose. At this stage the costing can also be checked.

∞ **links**

See Quality assurance, pages 66–67, to find out how to plan for quality.

See User trials and product comparison, pages 66–67, for further details on prototype testing.

See Production flowcharts, pages 112–113, to understand how quality control checks are included in production systems.

See Manufacturing specifications, pages 114–115, to learn about tolerance levels.

3 Production sampling

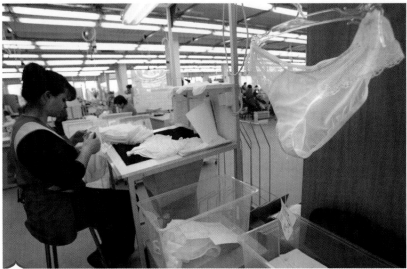

B *A quality control inspector at work*

During quality control inspections, a sample product is taken from the batch to check that it meets the manufacturing specification. If a fault is detected further products will be checked to see if there is a problem in the production line. A minor fault in an individual product can be put right to reduce the number of substandard products overall. Photo B shows an inspector measuring the garment length with a tape measure. Seam allowance will need to meet the tolerance levels described on the manufacturing specification.

Activities

1 Examine two or more identical pillowcases or cushion covers; or next time you buy a multiple pack of school shirts, pants, handkerchiefs, etc. lay out all the pieces. Measure the size, distance between fastenings or decorative motifs etc. and write down your results in a table.

2 Are the measurements of the identical products exactly the same or very slightly different from each other? The measurements might vary by only a few millimetres. Work out the differences and add this column to your table – these differences are within the tolerance levels.

Members of staff inspect products to check that no dangerous materials, such as pieces of broken needles have been trapped in the garment during manufacture. A metal detection machine is used to help workers ensure that the products are safe. On the factory floor broken needles are changed by a particular worker who checks and replaces them, counting needles in and out to reduce the risk of leaving any in the products.

Summary

Quality control is one aspect of quality assurance.

Checks are made to test the quality during different stages in the making of a product.

Feedback from quality control checks will help prevent faults from reoccurring.

8.1 Use of ICT for researching and sorting information

1 Design a questionnaire to find out popular styles of bag for young people aged 12–16.

a You will need to write a list of simple questions that will provide information about the types of bag that are popular. You should ask about style, colour and size preferences and how much each person would be willing to pay for a bag. You could also find out which materials are most popular, e.g. canvas, denim or nylon fabric.

b Ask about 10 young people to fill in your questionnaire.

c Only question your target market, so that your collected data is relevant.

d Use ICT to present the questionnaire, with tick boxes where appropriate.

e Collect results and use Excel to make graphs to draw conclusions from your research.

f Which bag style is the most popular with the target market?

Objectives

Consider how ICT can be used to help with research.

Appreciate the difference between primary and secondary research.

Understand how ICT can be used to sort data.

AQA Examiner's tip

Be able to explain the difference between primary and secondary research.

Primary research

A designer carries out primary research to collect information and inspiration. Looking at what the target market is buying, examining existing products, asking people's opinions and collecting pictures and samples are all second nature to the designer. A digital camera is an essential research tool; photos can be taken in shops, at exhibitions, on the street – anywhere that will help give design inspiration.

Questionnaires

Questionnaires can be designed to collect specific types of data. Open questions will be more difficult to answer by the respondent; data provided will be difficult to analyse as long sentences may be written, but answers may be very informative. Closed questions, where a choice of expected answers is given for the respondent to circle or tick, may get more results, as this style of question is easier to answer. Questionnaires can be printed or e-mailed to specific people.

Secondary research

The internet is a main source of research already put together by others. A designer can use **search engines** to find websites, images and videos that will broaden ideas and give a very wide choice of written and visual material to work from. Company websites, magazine

Key terms

Search engine: an internet tool to list web pages that feature the word or words entered in the search box.

and newspaper articles, TV broadcasts online and even blogs can give much valuable information. The internet is immediate, easy to update and accessible, perhaps making travel and conversation to find out information unnecessary. However, there is no guarantee that the information found on the internet is either valid or honest. Traditionally books, journals and catalogues have provided published material that is verified.

⬯⬯links

Find out more at **www.trendstop.com** see how fashion and colour trend forecasts are organised and sold to designers. See how designers get inspiration, page 56–57, to read about how designers use computers to research ideas.

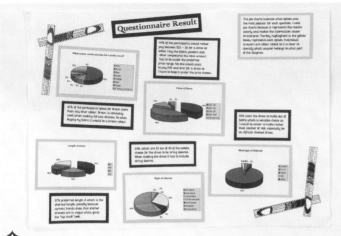

A *Temitayo analyses results from her questionnaire using ICT*

Remember

- The internet can provide fact or opinion, so use your collected information cautiously.
- You may need to ask permission from the shop owner if taking photos in a shop.

Databases and graphs

Although designers can buy material from online resource libraries, such as Trendstop.com, they usually also set up their own reference collection of photos and designs. Storage on computer hard disks may be quickly filled, so CD-ROMs may be used to store the library files.

Data can be presented using spreadsheets with graphs produced to analyse results. These can help to evaluate the research by providing visual impressions of the results.

B *Trendstop.com will sell images from its databases to designers who subscribe*

Summary

ICT will speed up research and provide a means to store, sort and present data.

Computers aid research and enable designers to organise reference material for future retrieval.

Companies exist to research information and provide it to those who pay to obtain collected and analysed research material.

Using computers to design and present

Computers are used by designers for:

- writing documents and display boards, including artwork, text, spreadsheets, graphs and tables
- supplementing drawing and colouring by hand; a quick pencil sketch or detailed painted illustration will often be completed to record ideas and communicate them to others, but ICT will sometimes be more appropriate
- putting together slide show presentations
- digital photography and video making
- designing and sampling.

Programs used by designers

These include:

- Microsoft Office – Word, Excel, PowerPoint, Publisher
- drawing packages – Paint, Adobe Illustrator, CorelDraw
- image editing – Photoshop
- specialist fashion software, e.g. Speed Step.

A A designer puts a presentation together for a client

Activities

1. Use a program such as 'Paint' to draw a design for a cushion cover or wall hanging, using autoshapes to provide the basis for the product line drawing. Try out available functions such as repeating, rotating or reflecting parts of the design to build up pattern in the final drawing.

2. Copy the line drawing three times. Take each copy in turn and fill in the colour, making three different colourways. Which colourway is the most effective? Explain why it is the most appealing.

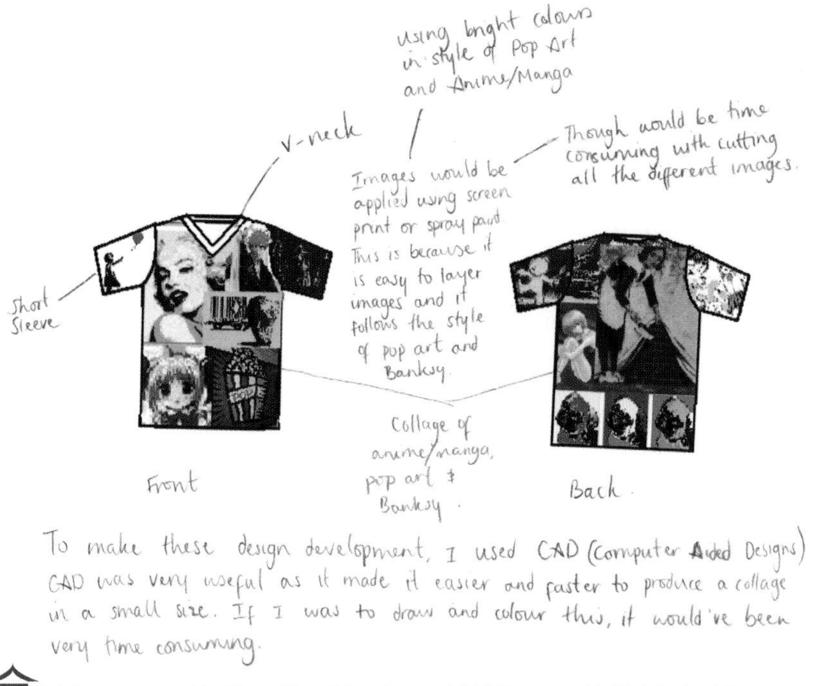
Using bright colours in style of Pop Art and Anime/Manga
V-neck
Images would be applied using screen print or spray paint. This is because it is easy to layer images and it follows the style of pop art and Banksy.
Though would be time consuming with cutting all the different images.
Short Sleeve
Collage of anime/manga, pop art & Banksy.
Front
Back
To make these design development, I used CAD (Computer Aided Designs). CAD was very useful as it made it easier and faster to produce a collage in a small size. If I was to draw and colour this, it would've been very time consuming.

B *Sylvia uses a combination of hand drawing and CAD to present initial design ideas*

Drawing using software

Drawing software can be used to design, illustrate and show working drawings. Drawn lines and shapes or photographic images can be imported and edited, or scanned to manipulate and develop ideas. Collections with a range of coordinating products can be developed from one initial idea.

With some specialist software it is possible to get a 3D impression of the design, by rotating the design and seeing it from different viewpoints. The designer can use the computer to simulate draping and shadowing to create a realistic image of the design. Also, ideas for different colourways can be tested and a variety of printed, knitted or woven fabric designs can be trialled on screen, to see the effect of each different combination of colour and texture.

Use of ICT for presentation

The designer can present ideas to the client on screen or printed on to presentation boards, or via e-mail, and then quickly modify them according to client feedback. Promotional material developed from design work can be adapted for use on websites, business stationery and advertising and marketing materials, such as point-of-sale literature and display posters. Computers make this development of related design work a quicker process.

Designing and sampling using computers

Computers can be used to pass detailed design information to machinery quickly so that samples can be made during the design and development stages, often without the designers even leaving their workstations:

links

See Using machines in textile production, pages 98–99, for information about computerised machines.

- Designers can use computers to design new woven or knitted fabrics on screen, and then show the new fabric in use on a drawn model, on screen or on printed copy.
- Printed fabric designs developed on screen can be digitally printed on to actual fabric for sampling.
- Embroidered motifs and patterns can be designed on the computer and then stitched directly on to fabric.

A design process that previously took weeks or months can now take less than 24 hours. The images on colour monitors and those reproduced by colour printers are so realistic that they can be used to present ideas to fashion buyers. In the past buyers have demanded to see and touch actual sample garments, before deciding to place orders, but with the new computer technology they now have the confidence to buy from screened or printed presentations.

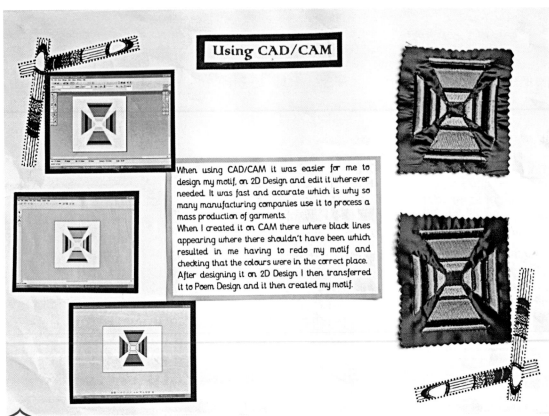

Using CAD/CAM

When using CAD/CAM it was easier for me to design my motif, on 2D Design and edit it wherever needed. It was fast and accurate which is why so many manufacturing companies use it to process a mass production of garments.
When I created it on CAM there where black lines appearing where there shouldn't have been which resulted in me having to redo my motif and checking that the colours were in the correct place. After designing it on 2D Design I then transferred it to Poem Design and it then created my motif.

C Temitayo uses the computer to design and embroider an African-inspired motif to embellish her dress

Tootal

The company Tootal supplies fabric for men's shirts. The company has invested a large amount of money in computers that can be used by designers to create new fabric designs quickly. Compare the system used in the past with the present-day system that uses **CAD**.

D Tootal men's shirt

In the past

- In Manchester, the fabric designer sketched out a weave plan on graph paper, and selected colours from a chart provided by the yarn makers.
- A skilled painter would then copy the design on to a piece of cardboard.
- The painted design was sent to Japan, to the weaving mill, where the cost of making the woven fabric would be worked out.
- Samples were shown to buyers from Britain's major department stores, which are based in London.
- If the sample was approved, the mill in Japan bought the yarns and began weaving.

Today, using CAD

- Using a computer, the designers select a weave pattern and the yarn colours, which are linked to individual yarns in the mill's stock in Japan, and then they watch an image of the fabric appear on their monitors.
- They can modify the design – make the stripe a bit narrower or wider, the colour a bit deeper or paler, or change one background colour to another one – before printing a paper copy of the new fabric design for senior directors to inspect.
- After approval, the design is sent over the telecommunications network to an identical computer and printer at the mill in Japan.
- When the costing comes back, the design is sent using the computer to Tootal's London office, which provides the buyers with screenings or printouts of the design.

The use of computers has made it possible to design fabric more quickly. Buyers can now have a closer partnership with designers, to work together to develop fabric that is fine-tuned to the needs of the customer.

See www.tootal.uk for further information.

Remember

Computers often speed up designing and presentation but both computer-aided design (CAD) and hand techniques should be made use of as appropriate.

AQA Examiner's tip

- Be able to list a wide variety of uses of ICT in design and presentation.
- Explain how some programs can benefit the designer.

Summary

Photography, scanning, and drawing provide starting points for designing.

Computers can make a presentation easier and quicker to put together and send to the client.

Working drawings and illustrations can be stored for future use, when drawings can be modified for new designs.

Designing is directly linked to sample making, on screen, on printouts or on actual fabric.

Use of computerised systems and machinery

Computers are used throughout design and making activities in companies. Once computer systems and computerised machinery are in place, they increase efficiency, consistency and accuracy. Time can be saved and modifications made more easily. Production can be closely monitored for quality and safety, and costs reduced due to efficiency. The following list outlines where **CAM** benefits the manufacturer:

- Pattern design, grading (making different sizes of pattern) and pattern making can be computer aided.
- Pattern lay plans are worked out using a computer plan. The lay plan ensures that the pattern pieces are laid out close together, in the most efficient way to reduce fabric wastage.
- Digital printing on to fabric is done for sampling and for the full production run.
- Computer controlled weaving looms – designs can be quickly altered on the computer linked to the loom.
- Individual seamless knitted garments can be made from instructions sent by the computer linked to the knitting machine. Knitted fabric designs can be quickly altered on the computer linked to the machine.
- automatic spreading of fabric and cutting out.
- Sewing machines can be programmed to perform tasks such as making buttonholes and attaching pockets.
- Labelling is done as part of product tracking through the production line; the design and making of the garment label may be computerised.

Computers also assist with:

- monitoring of quality
- fabric warehousing and stock control, using bar codes to enable just-in-time (JIT) stock control
- Production scheduling to monitor time schedules and flow through production process.

Lectra

Lectra is a company that provides integrated technology solutions (software, CAD/CAM equipment and associated services) to the fashion industry. Computers can be used to create and test designs; patterns can be developed, prototypes made and production runs completed. The link between designing and manufacturing is very close.

A *A designer uses ICT to design a new collection showing fabric choice and colourways*

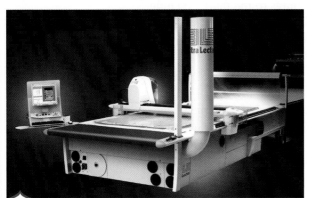

B *Fabric design is printed digitally so that a sample can be made in the selected fabric, it is then sent to the manufacturing area where products are made and dispatched*

What advantages does this close link between CAD/CAM bring to the designers?

Summary

Computers can be used to increase efficiency and accuracy in manufacturing.

Costs can be reduced if efficiency is increased.

Health and safety of workers can be monitored and working conditions made safer using computers.

Flexibility is increased as changes in production can be made more rapidly.

AQA *Examiner's tip*

Be clear about the benefits of using CAM.

AQA Examination-style questions

Question 1 is about industrial production systems and is the type of question you would expect to see in Section B of the written paper.

1   (a)   What are the three main types of production system?   *(3 marks)*
    (b)   Explain in detail why it is important to plan for production.   *(3 marks)*
    (c)   During production some parts of products might be made as a sub-assembly.
          Explain what is meant by a sub-assembly?   *(3 marks)*
    (d)   Explain what is meant by just–in–time stock control (JIT).   *(2 marks)*
    (e)   Draw a simple flowchart to show how to make the following products:
          (i)   Cushion cover with a zip fastening
          (ii)   T-Shirt
          (iii) Skirt   *(6 marks for each flow chart)*
    (f)   (i)   What is a manufacturing specification?   *(3 marks)*
          (ii)   Give 6 pieces of information that could be included on a manufacturing
                 specification.   *(6 marks)*

Question 2 is about techniques and processes and is the type of question you would expect to see in Section B of the written paper.

2   (a)   Name two different fastenings used on textile products. Use notes and
          diagrams to explain how to add these fastenings to the fabric. Include
          information about materials and equipment that will be needed.   *(6 marks)*
    (b)   Many textile products include pockets. Explain one method of constructing a
          pocket and of attaching it to a wall hanging.
          Use notes and diagrams to show how this could be done step-by-step.   *(6 marks)*
    (c)   (i)   List three different ways to neaten a flat seam.   *(3 marks)*
          (ii)   Use notes and diagrams to explain one method of neatening a flat seam.
                 Include information about materials and equipment that will be needed. *(6 marks)*
    (d)   List 3 different hand tools for cutting.   *(3 marks)*
    (e)   A dart is often made in textile products. What is a dart?   *(2 marks)*
    (f)   Use notes and diagrams to show how a dart could be put into a piece of fabric. *(6 marks)*
    (g)   Use notes and diagrams to explain one method of inserting a zip.
          Include information about materials and equipment that will be needed. *(6 marks)*
    (h)   Use notes and diagrams to explain one method of making a button hole.
          Include information about materials and equipment that will be needed. *(6 marks)*

Question 3 is about computer technology and communication and is the type of question you would expect to see in Section B of the written paper.

3   (a)   Explain how ICT can be used to research, collect, sort and present information.   *(2 marks)*
    (b)   Computers can be used by designers to help them design and present ideas.
          Give two advantages when using them to draw fashion designs.   *(2 marks)*
    (c)   List three ways that computers can be used in textile manufacturing and explain
          how their use benefits production.   *(6 marks)*

AQA Examination-style questions

Examiner's tip

- Show your knowledge and understanding by explaining which particular tools, equipment, machines and methods of working are appropriate for the specific product mentioned in the question.

- Use pencil diagrams with written notes to explain what you mean, if it helps to show your knowledge and understanding.

- Always explain the benefits of using computers, rather than just saying 'use CAD/CAM'.

- Remember, design ideas will need to be modified for industrial manufacture.

- Production planning includes quality assurance.

Introduction

■ What is Designing and making practice?

A GCSE grade for Textiles technology is achieved by completing two units:

■ Unit 1   A written paper worth 40 per cent of the total marks.

■ Unit 2   A coursework project which is worth 60 per cent of the total marks. This project will enable you to show your designing and making skills and therefore is called Designing and making practice. It is assessed to the 'Controlled assessment criteria' shown below:

1 Investigating the design context

2 Development of design proposals

3 Making

4 Testing and evaluation

5 Communication.

The five criteria together are worth 90 marks.

Your designing and making project must meet strict guidelines, hence the name ' Controlled assessment'.

A successful project will show that you have followed a design process and will show evidence that you have met the assessment criteria set out by the examination board.

You will have approximately 45 hours to carry out this task. This may seem a long time, but you will need every minute of that time to:

■ choose and analyse the task

■ plan, carry out research and then analyse your findings

■ write the design criteria or specification

■ create and evaluate ideas

■ develop the ideas and present a final design

■ write a product specification

■ plan and make the product

■ test and evaluate the product.

■ Guidelines for the completion of a task

■ You need to be familiar with the way that your project will be marked. This is called a scheme of assessment.

■ The scheme of assessment shows how many marks are available for each part of your work. It also describes the sort of things you need to include in each section.

■ Your teacher has to be certain that the work you submit for the controlled assessment has been done by you. For this reason most of it has to be done in the classroom. You can ask other people for opinions as part of your research, e.g. asking people what they think of your design ideas, or what they think of the product you have designed. You cannot submit other people's design work.

- Your design work can be produced on paper or electronically. If you do your designing electronically, PowerPoint works well. You could also create a single PDF file that contains your whole design folder. Either of these methods allows an examiner to look through your work easily.

- Your teacher will give you a design task or list of possible tasks. You will need to choose a task that interests you. You are likely to be working on this project for several months!

Some points to help you present the work

- You need to plan your work carefully – spend a maximum of 45 hours on it.

- Space on pages needs to be used well – every mark should be communicating something special.

- Your folder should consist of 20–25 sides of A3 paper.

- Show your creativity through an individual style of presentation.

- The size of your writing/font size needs to be legible.

- You need to keep all research information concise.

- Keep focused on the task – the folder should show your design thinking at every stage.

- The quality of presentation of your ideas should be inspirational.

- The quality of your written communication needs to accurate.

- Use the correct technical language.

- Make full use of the computer at all stages.

- Photographs are an excellent sources of evidence of your 'making skills'.

Your questions answered

■ How should I present my work?

It is a good idea to discuss presentation with your teacher. A3 is a good size to present your work because it gives you plenty of space to show the flow of your ideas. A4 can be restrictive. A plastic folder protects your work from dust and damage; it is also easy to send to the moderator.

■ Do I have to do all my work on the computer?

No. You need to think about the purpose of each piece of work and choose the most effective way of presenting it. Presenting work such as an analysis or an evaluation report should be done on the computer,

whereas a working, thinking document with mind maps or initial ideas can be done by hand.

Does all the writing need to be word processed?

No; however, Criterion 5 assesses your written communication skills, so word processing could ensure that your work has text that is legible, easily understood and shows good spelling, punctuation and grammar.

Do I have to use a computerised sewing machine?

It is a good idea to use all the modern technology available in your school. If you have a machine in your school and it is the best way of doing the task then use it.

Can I put all my work on to a PowerPoint presentation and submit it to the moderator?

Yes, but you do need to have your teacher's agreement as they will have to let the examination board know. This is becoming a popular way of presenting work.

How much should I put in the task folder?

The design folder should consist of approximately 20–25 sides of A3 paper or the sketchbook equivalent. The space on each page should be used well and writing should be concise and accurate.

How much time should be spent on the task?

The complete project including all design work and all making work should take no more than 45 hours.

Can I complete any of the work at home?

Your teacher has to be certain that you have done the work. You will still do homework: gathering research and drafting out pieces of work are two examples. Any work that the teacher is not sure is yours will not gain you marks.

Can I write my own time-controlled task?

No. You must use a brief which has been set by the awarding body (AQA) and given to you by your teacher. You may be given several briefs to choose from.

■ I have been on a workshop out of school. Can I use this work in my folder?

No. The teacher who is marking your work must be able to sign to say they saw you doing it. However, it could be entered as a useful piece of research work.

■ Can I use a commercial pattern?

Yes. It is important to design original ideas that are perfect for the intended user. When you have developed your ideas you will need to find the best way of making the paper template. It could be by adapting a commercial pattern, drafting your own or by disassembling an existing product.

■ How many modifications do I have to make to the commercial pattern?

There is no set number. Remember that the product you make must be original, show your skills and have a high level of demand if you are going to gain the highest marks. Buying a basic commercial pattern and making it up is not going to do this.

■ What happens if I copy an existing design?

You will not gain the highest marks and you are not likely to enjoy the task. Designers should use existing designs to inspire new ideas that are different and more fashionable and to improve the design.

■ Do I need to include photographic evidence?

It is very good practice to show evidence of the completed product in use as it helps with the testing and evaluating process. Many students find it useful to record the making process through a photographic diary.

■ Who will mark my work?

Your teacher will assess everything you have done; this includes all work in your design folder and the final made product. A moderator from the AQA will request some or all of the Textiles technology work from your school and will re-mark it trying to agree your teacher's marks. You will then be awarded a mark for your Designing and making practice which will be added to the mark you get for the written examination. Your final grade will then be calculated.

9 Investigating the design opportunity

9.1 Analysis of the task

Design contexts and controlled assessment tasks

The examination board will provide a set of controlled assessment tasks. You will choose one with the help of your teacher.

Example of a design context

Designers have a responsibility to design products that address environmental issues; they may be inspired by:

- designing for sustainability
- recycled and second-hand textile products
- used fabrics and components
- vintage fabrics
- organic cotton
- fabrics from other industrial sources, e.g. tarpaulin from lorries, hessian from rice sacks, biodegradable fibres/fabrics
- ethical trading.

Examples of controlled assessment tasks

Design task 1

Current trend forecasts show that the Japanese Street Style is set to influence fashion in the near future. This trend lends itself to the creation of garments which make use of recycled textile products, materials and components. You have been commissioned by a popular high street store to design a fashion garment or accessory which reflects this influence.

Design task 2

Design and make a fashion garment or accessory suitable for the 18–23 year age range taking your inspiration from either 'The Age of Punk' or the 'Swinging Sixties'. If the product is successful it will form part of a limited range to be sold at Music Festivals throughout the country.

Analysing the task

Some points to help you get started

- You have to show that you understand what the task involves.
- Highlight the key words in the task.
- A mind map using the key words from the brief is a good starting point.
- Write down what you need to know before you can start designing.
- Plan the research activities.

A *Japanese street style*

B *Inspired by the age of punk*

Objectives

Understand how to analyse the task.

Understand how to identify research activities.

◯◯ links

Find out more at

www.aqa.org.uk

the AQA web site has a full list of the controlled assessment tasks, criteria and the different mark bands.

Katie is designing and making a wall hanging inspired by the theme of Africa. It is to be produced in quantity and sold in a modern home furnishings store.

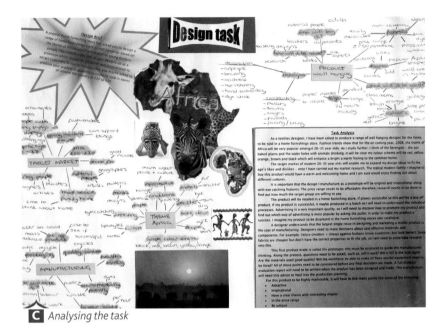

 Analysing the task

Sarah is designing and making a cushion as part of a range of bedroom furnishings for a modern family home. She has been inspired by the Chinese culture and the red, gold and black colour range.

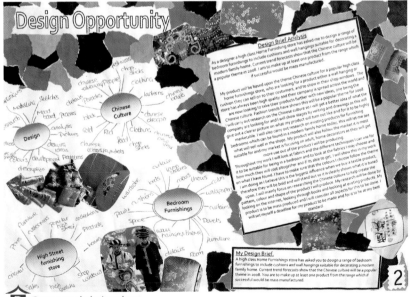

D *Coursework design sheet*

 AQA Examiner's comment
Sarah's early thinking is presented in the form of mind maps and the written analysis shows good understanding. It is clear that she has identified areas of research to support her designing.

AQA Examiner's comment
Katie has shown that she understands what the assessment task is asking her to do. The inspirational theme of Africa is presented well through the images. It is important to show the examiner the process you go through when analysing, so she has highlighted the key words and set out her thinking in the form of mind maps. Being an able student she has gone on to produce an extended piece of writing in a clear and coherent manner. This thorough analysis highlights the aspects that will need research if the outcome is going to be inspirational.

AC5 communication

- Excellent, appropriate presentation, with good use of the space.
- Handwritten mind maps are a good way of getting your ideas down quickly.
- The student is aiming for a high grade so needs to communicate her higher-level thinking skills. An extended piece of writing is the best way to do this.

AC5 communication

- The information is clear though there is a slight over-decoration of the sheet.
- The text has been printed on white paper, which makes it easier for the examiner to read.

Summary

You should now be able to:

analyse a controlled assessment task

identify research activities.

Design b...
As a designer a high class Home Furnishing store has aske...
bedroom furnishings to include cushions and wall hangings suitable for...
modern family home. Current trend forecasts show that the Chinese culture will be
...me in 2008. I am to make up at least one product from the range which
...cessful would be mass manufactured.
...re for a popular high class
...hanging or ...

9.2 Research

Research and its analysis may take place at any stage of the design process. When you are developing the final product you may have to do further research to help you decide on such things as fabric choice or the best techniques to use.

What is the purpose of initial research?

- To inspire product shape and style.
- To give ideas for colour ranges.
- To provide pattern.
- To understand the customer/consumer.
- To consider what will be fashionable and be in the right price range.
- To give some idea of products that could sell well.
- To gain an understanding of construction and decorative techniques used in textile products.
- To have an insight into fabrics that have been used successfully in the past.

Research – planning

- Think about the purpose of the initial research you are going to do.
- Look at your analysis of the task and decide what you need to find out in order to start designing.
- You have little time – plan what research needs to be carried out.
- You will carry out further research as you develop the product.

Objectives

Understand how to select relevant research.

Understand how to carry out detailed research.

⊙⊙ links

See Chapter 4 Product analysis and evaluation on techniques.

AC5 communication

- The images have been chosen carefully to give colour, pattern, shapes and texture.
- The presentation is individual; the sheet is very full but is not messy.

A *Research planning chart*

Research	How?	Why?
The theme	Visit – take photographs. Produce a mood or theme board	To inspire and give ideas for colour, style, pattern, shape
Existing designs	Comparative shop	To see how products are constructed
	Internet	To give ideas about fabrics, techniques
	Disassembly task	To consider what makes the product popular
	Product analysis	To understand value for money
Target market	Talk to the people who are likely to buy or use your product. Find out about them as this will guide you when you come up with ideas	These people are going to buy the product so you must know their needs and tastes
Shop profile	Visit the place of sale	Your product must fit in with the style of the shop and be in the right price range and suit the kinds of customers who visit the shop
	Look at the internet site or catalogue	

Research – carrying it out

- Only collect research data that you need in order to give you ideas.
- Keep asking yourself, 'What information do I need to get me started designing?'

- Look in a wide range of places for the information. Avoid just using the internet.
- Be focused and only present the very best material that you are going to use.

Iona is designing and making a fashion corset for the 18–35-year-old age range. The designs will be inspired by animal prints and will be marketed by an exclusive mail order catalogue 'Lazaza'.

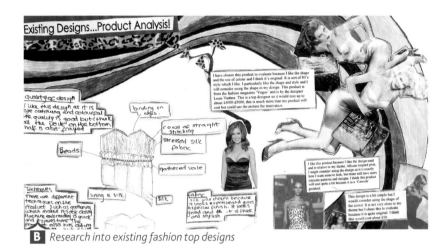

B *Research into existing fashion top designs*

Anna is designing and making a cushion for students at university away from home and living in rented accommodation. The cushions, based on a musical theme, will be sold in a campus shop raising money for charity.

C *A mood or theme board*

AQA Examiner's comment	Iona has researched fashion tops. Her evaluative comments are brief though she is clearly looking to inform her own designing. A detailed product analysis has been done on a corset similar to the one she hopes to design. The quality of the design, fabrics and components used, techniques employed and fastenings have all been analysed. Iona has picked out those things that are going to inspire her and she is very focused on the design task ahead.

AC5 communication

- Presentation is good and the theme of animal prints is carried through.
- Communication about the designs and their value is good.
- Existing designs from magazines and the internet have been chosen wisely.
- An existing design has been sketched and shows good observation skills.
- Spontaneous thoughts about the design are handwritten, which is an appropriate method of communicating this information.

AQA Examiner's comment	Anna has put together a mood or theme board based on musical instruments. Some are close up and detailed, while others are distance shots where the focus is shape. A red, black and metallic colour scheme gives a message that this is likely to be popular with young people, as it is modern and likely to sell well.

Summary

You should now be able to:

carry out relevant research

put a mood or theme board together

evaluate existing designs.

Design Brief
As a designer a high class Home Furnishing store has asked...
bedroom furnishings to include cushions and wall hangings suitable for...
modern family home. Current trend forecasts show that the Chinese culture will be
...ome in 2008. I am to make up at least one product from the range which
...cessful would be mass manufactured.
...ure for a popular high class
...II hanging or...

9.3 Research analysis

Analysing your research

1 You have completed your research and presented it – you must now analyse it and say what you have found out.

2 The examiner will need to see:

- what research you have done
- why you did it
- what you hoped to find out
- what you actually found out; and
- how you are going to use it in your design work.

3 The table below will help you get started.

Some points to help you

- You may not have researched something because you already knew the information. Make sure you let the examiner know.

- When you have planned the analysis complete the extended piece of writing.

- In the first paragraph say what your design brief is asking you to do.

- Then say what you needed to find out, followed by the research you have carried out.

- Explain why you needed to do the research. This could be anything from looking for inspiration, to gaining knowledge of something you did not know.

- In the final paragraph summarise your findings. Let the examiner know what you are thinking. How might your product develop? Be clear, honest and open.

Objectives

Understand how to analyse your research findings.

Understand how to write a design specification.

∞ links

See Chapter 4 Product analysis and evaluation on techniques.

A *Analysing the research*

RESEARCH	What did you hope to find out?	What key things did you discover?	Examples of design criteria
Mood board	Ideas for colour, style, pattern, shape	Describe your mood board followed by the colour, patterns and shapes you have taken from it. What are your early thoughts?	The colour range will be green, blue and yellow The pattern from the Gaudi tiles will form the background
Consumer profile: public survey, market research	Their likes and dislikes, how much they are prepared to spend	Describe the customer who will buy your product and say why you need information about them. What did you find out? What do you think they will buy? How much do you think they will spend?	The product must appeal to young couples it must be modern and fashionable
Shop profile	The type of products the shop sells. Price ranges. Customer types	What did you find out about the shop? What kinds of products do they sell? How will this have an effect on your designs?	The product will sell in the £20–£40 price range
Existing designs: internet, shops, magazines	Product construction Ideas about fabrics, techniques The popular products What is value for money?	You have presented some existing products with full written evaluations. What have you found out? How will you use this idea in your work? Write as much as you can; there is no right and wrong, it is just what you think	The product will be square and have a decorative edging Hand-stitched decorative work will be involved

Writing the design specification

A design specification is a detailed list of criteria, which provide information needed to design a product.

It is written to guide the designers' thinking. Use it to steer you in the right direction as you come up with ideas. You will need to use it when you evaluate your ideas

Some points to help you

Look at your analysis draft chart. The end column will be your starting point when writing the specification. It shows that you have used the analysis when identifying the specification criteria.

These are some of the criteria you might include in your design specification:

- function/purpose
- aesthetics
- target market/consumer requirements
- products in the season's range
- performance requirements
- time and resources
- value issues – moral, environmental, sustainability, social
- details (if decisions have been made) on style, size
- health and safety issues
- life expectancy
- scale of production.

Amanda is designing and making a bag inspired by an Indian pattern with the 16–24-year-old target market in mind.

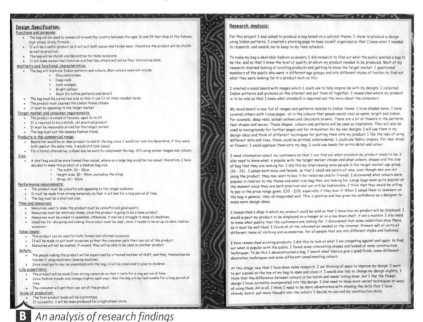

B *An analysis of research findings*

AQA Examiner's comment

Amanda has produced a detailed analysis of her research findings. Not all her work, such as the opinions of others and her knowledge of techniques, has been presented in the folder, but she has explained how this knowledge will influence her. She describes the research carried out, why she did it and finally what she actually found out. The most able students will explain how their findings are going to influence their designing. The analysis is reflected in the very detailed design specification presented.

AC5 communication

- Excellent, appropriate presentation of the information. Neat with no decoration.
- It is clear how the research is going to be used.
- The design criteria are detailed and will be of great value during designing.

Summary

You should now be able to:

analyse your research

write a design specification.

10.1 Design ideas 1

This is the most exciting part of your coursework.

The purpose of the task is to design something new, original and exciting, a product with a difference, something that everyone will want to buy!

- You have carried out some initial research in order to inspire you – make sure you use it!

- You have written a design specification – let it guide your thinking.

- Your ideas must be wide-ranging, original, exciting. It is no good copying someone else's work or tracing out commercial patterns.

- All ideas must be well presented. The thinking behind your ideas must be clear and the examiner must be in no doubt what the product is.

Initial sketched ideas

- Using an HB or 2B pencil, sketch out some early ideas. If you find it hard to get going have a look at how existing products work and choose a product design that appeals to you. Now look at your image board and pick out some patterns and shapes that you like. Combine the two.

- Be bold and confident. Relax and sketch freely. Don't use erasers, rulers, coloured pencils or compasses. You must let your ideas flow.

- Let the moderator see what you are thinking. Make notes if your drawings are not too clear.

- Don't spend too long on this stage. One hour is quite long enough!

Andrew is designing and making a fashion bag for the 18–35-year-old female target group. The bag will form part of a summer range inspired by the theme of flowers.

Objectives

Understand how to sketch initial ideas.

Understand how to present original, imaginative ideas.

∞ links

See How designers get inspired, pages 56–57

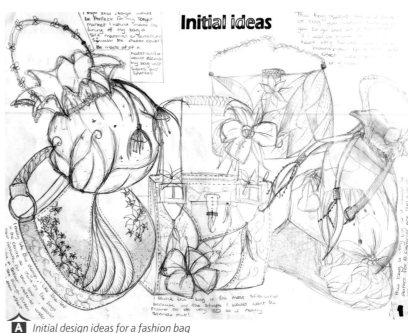

Initial ideas

A *Initial design ideas for a fashion bag*

B   *Initial ideas for a mood board*

Andrew has sketched original ideas for the bag, taking inspiration from existing designs and his mood board. The mood board is inspirational and provides the colour, pattern and shapes needed to help Andrew with his designs. His ideas are imaginative, reflect the theme of lilies and are marketable products. He shows his artistic flair and sketches in a bold, confident manner. The evaluations are limited, though this is acceptable during the early stages of designing.

Zoë is designing and making an evening dress for the 18–35-year-old female target group. The dress will form part of a summer range inspired by the sea and the movement of the waves.

C   *Initial ideas for an evening dress*

AC5 communication

- The communication of ideas is excellent and ideas are seen to flow freely.

Zoë has decided to design and make an evening dress, which is very ambitious in the time allowed for this project. Unless she has lots of experience of making garments she may find the making a real challenge. The ideas presented are fairly basic and other than the wave pattern offer little originality. They are well drawn and the annotation gives some idea of style and techniques. Candidates would be expected to produce more than four initial ideas if they are aiming for the higher grades.

AC5 communication

- The initial ideas are well presented and the shape and style of the dress clear.
- Annotation could have been written freehand on this early working sheet.

Summary

You should now be able to:

present your initial ideas.

Coloured ideas

- You must now firm up your ideas and present some realistic suggestions. Remember the basic design principles – shape, style, colour, pattern, balance, proportion.

- Do not waste time designing things you know you will never want to develop and make.

- Do some exploded diagrams to show details. Show the back views.

- It is a good idea to present your developing ideas in colour.

- Keep your mind open. You may decide to combine two of your first ideas. As you are working you may suddenly hit on a really good new idea.

- You must evaluate your designs! How do they meet the design specification?

- Remember there are lots of ways to come up with ideas. Try exploring with fabrics, use a paint-and-draw or a photo software package or model with paper.

Maddie is designing a summer skirt that will be influenced by Japanese culture and its use of flowers.

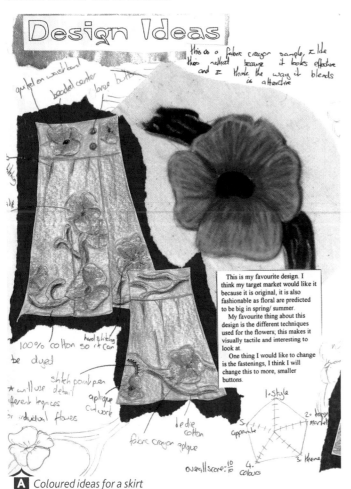

A *Coloured ideas for a skirt*

AQA Examiner's comment

The ideas are presented well by Maddie and she shows both the front and back views of the skirt. They are evaluated well against the specification criteria and we can see achievable designs in the time available. Details of technique possibilities have been highlighted though Maddie recognises that further experimentation will be needed when the skirt design is developed. An idea for a flower motif has been trialled on fabric using dye crayons.

AC5 communication

- The ideas are presented well, though the use of colour is weak on two of the designs.

- Annotation is fluent and design thinking clear.

- The star diagrams are useful in giving a quick evaluation.

Gemma is designing a wall hanging that will be influenced by the vibrant colours and images of Hawaii.

B *Coloured ideas for a wall hanging*

AQA
Examiner's comment

Look how the mood board images of Hawaii have influenced Gemma's designing. The ideas are complex, reflect the theme and are appropriate for the customer requirements. The evaluations are very detailed and show whether or not the individual designs meet the requirements of the design specification. Handwritten annotation labels the fabrics, threads and techniques that could be used.

Sarah is designing and making an evening dress for the 18–35-year-old female target group. The dress will form part of a summer range inspired by insects.

C *Ideas from fabrics and threads*

AQA
Examiner's comment

Sarah has been very ambitious in tackling the making of an evening dress in the time allowed. The idea presented on this sheet stems from working on an appliquéd textile sample. Doing this has given her the idea to include an appliquéd band on a very basic dress design. Without this experimenting she is unlikely to have hit upon this achievable design idea. Not all students come up with the best ideas when drawing. Experimenting with paper, fabric, thread, colour and different techniques often gives the most original work.

AC5 communication

- The mood board is made up of carefully chosen images that are displayed artistically.
- The ideas are presented well, making good use of all the space.

AC5 communication

- The front and back of the design are well drawn and watercolour paints have been used successfully to add the colour.
- There is a clear explanation about the designs and the techniques used.

Summary

You should now be able to:

use your research

present imaginative and innovative coloured ideas

demonstrate creativity, flair and originality

consider alternative ways of coming up with ideas

evaluate your ideas against the design specification.

Planning

- This is the most important and time-consuming stage of your task.
- You will not have time to spend more than six hours on this so planning every stage is important.
- Present all your work on no more than eight A3 sheets.

Developing your ideas

- Choose the idea or ideas that come closest to meeting your specification.
- Look at the shape of the product – refine it, alter it! Is it going to do its job well if it is this shape?
- Look at patterns, decoration – rearrange, add new, try different. Is it fussy? Is the overall composition good?
- Think about the colours. Are they going to be fashionable? Do they reflect the season's trend? Experiment. Try different colourways.
- Make a paper model of the product. Is it the right size and shape? Imagine the decoration in place. Will it work?
- Think about how it will all fit together. Try out different construction techniques to find the best way of doing things. Make a mock-up or just part of the product.
- Make a paper pattern or template. Add all markings.
- Investigate ways of adding the colour and decoration.
- Choose fabrics. It is a good idea to list all the things the fabric must be if it is going to be suitable for your product, e.g. non stretchy, washable. If you are not sure about the fabric properties, you may have to test it.
- Choose the components, including threads and fastenings. See what is in the shops, test things out and make sure they give the right effect and do their job.
- Costing – now you have made decisions on the above, check that the product is still within your cost range.
- Mass manufacture – make a list of all the changes you might have to make if your product was to be mass produced.
- Think about the aftercare needed and the design of a care label.
- Consider health and safety issues. Is the product safe to make and also safe to use?
- Sustainability and other environmental, moral and social issues need considering when you are a designer and manufacturer.
- Present your final idea and seek public opinion. Write a product specification.

Objectives

Understand how to develop a design strategy.

Understand how to show evidence that you have used a planned approach throughout.

links

See Research, pages 136–137.

Maddie is designing a summer skirt that will be influenced by the flower motifs common in Japanese culture.

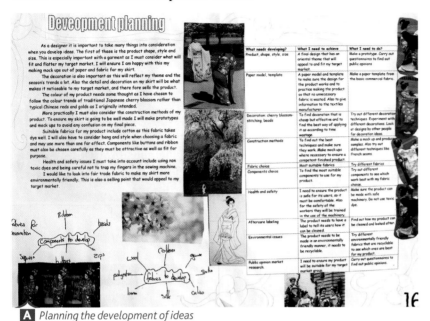

Gemma is designing a wall hanging that will be influenced by the vibrant colours and images of Hawaii.

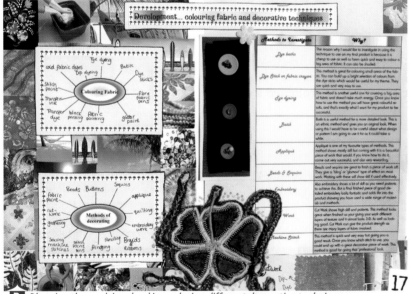

B *Planning the work involved in exploring different decorative techniques*

 AQA **Examiner's comment** This piece of work is evidence that Gemma is using a planned approach throughout the project. She recognises how short time is and so plans every stage of her work. She is focused on finding out which are the best techniques to use when she decorates the wall hanging. She knows she will have to impress the examiner by using some techniques that are demanding in skill. The two mind maps looked at all the possibilities and then she chose the ones that might suit her design. The table shows her reasons for carrying out these investigations. The machine-decorated motif is outstanding and shows high-level stitching skills. A second sheet of samples explores techniques further.

AC5 communication

■ Design thinking is clearly communicated in a fluent piece of writing.

■ Excellent presentation showing inspirational images without being fussy and over-decorating.

AQA **Examiner's comment** Maddie has explained her design thinking in an extended piece of writing. It is an open and honest reflection on the work carried out so far and what her design intentions are. It is a good idea to do this at regular intervals throughout the project as it gives the examiner a clear picture of your design thinking. Mind maps record her early thoughts about fabrics and components. The chart shows what Maddie needs to develop and what she is hoping to achieve. This is a planning document and helps students to focus on the most essential pieces of development work.

AC5 communication

■ The information on the design sheet is presented well, showing both planning and design thinking skills.

■ The cut-and-paste pictures are used as a background collage and offer further inspiration to the student.

Summary

You should now be able to:

understand what the 'development of ideas' means

plan the development work you need to do.

How to develop your product's shape and style

- Look at the ideas you have come up with so far. You will have a favourite!
- Go through every criterion on the design specification and see if it matches what you have designed.
- Now sketch your best idea, making modifications as you go.
- At this stage you need to concentrate on the shape and style of the product. It needs to be right for your customer target group.
- People are more likely to buy the product if it is fashionable and meets current trends so refine it, alter it until it does!
- Make a paper model of the product. Is it the right size and shape?
- In industry a designer would use a basic block pattern and work on adapting it. You can buy a commercial pattern and do the same thing.
- Think about how it will all fit together. Try out different construction techniques to find the best way of doing things.
- Make a mock-up or toile to confirm your ideas and check that it works.
- Remember it is your responsibility as a designer to make sure you have considered sustainability and other environmental, moral and social issues.
- Finally ask yourself – will it sell?
- Make a paper pattern or template. Add all markings.

Sarah is designing and making an evening dress for the 18–35-year-old female target group. The dress will form part of a summer range inspired by insects. You will have looked at one of her coloured ideas on page 143.

Have another look at Sarah's idea for her dress on page 143. Notice how she goes on to develop the style in the work shown on page 146.

Objectives

Understand how to develop the product shape and style.

Understand how to construct the product.

Understand how to present appropriate construction samples.

AC5 communication

- There is excellent communication of ideas through the quality of the drawings.
- Time is not wasted by colouring in at this stage.
- Written annotation is lacking though public opinion has been sought and a brief evaluation given.

AQA Examiner's comment

Have another look at Sarah's idea for her dress on page 143. Notice how she goes on to develop the style in the work shown on page 146. Insects have been a great source of inspiration as she designs the skirt. She has asked the public what they think of these ideas and has taken their comments on board. The evaluation of each design is weak though she does go on to give a very full comment later in the project before she makes her final decisions.

A *Design ideas for an insect inspired dress*

Joanne is designing a fashion top to be sold in an exclusive boutique. She has taken her inspiration from the Edwardian era.

⚬⚬ **links**

See Design ideas 2, pages 142–143 for Sarah's dress ideas.

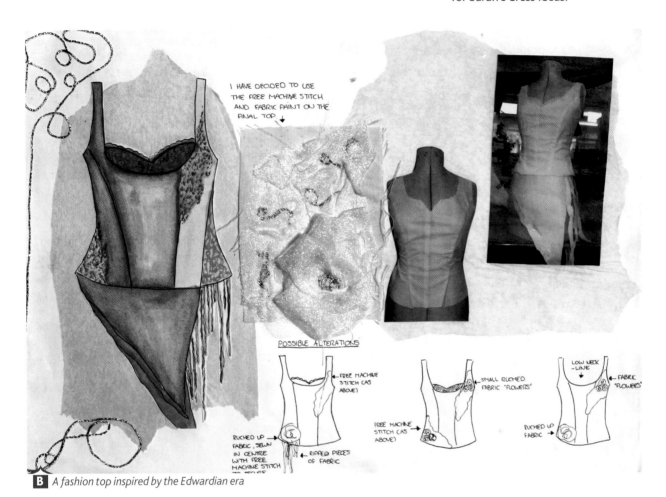

I HAVE DECIDED TO USE THE FREE MACHINE STITCH AND FABRIC PAINT ON THE FINAL TOP

POSSIBLE ALTERATIONS

FREE MACHINE STITCH (AS ABOVE)

RUCHED UP FABRIC, SEWN IN CENTRE WITH FREE MACHINE STITCH

RIPPED PIECES OF FABRIC

SMALL RUCHED FABRIC "FLOWERS"

FREE MACHINE STITCH (AS ABOVE)

LOW NECK –LINE

FABRIC "FLOWERS"

RUCHED UP FABRIC

B *A fashion top inspired by the Edwardian era*

AQA Examiner's comment The watercolour design shows how Joanne intends the top to look. You can see the calico toile she has made and how she is using paper to model the extension. The sketches at the bottom show she is exploring different ideas for the style of the upper part of the bodice. There is a lack of explanation about the stages she is going through as she develops the shape of the top and there is no indication of the back view.

AC5 communication

- The design sheet is presented neatly though written communication is poor.

Summary

You will now be able to:

develop the shape of your product

make a model or toile

investigate construction techniques and evaluate their use.

■ Colour

- You will have produced a mood board and your work will show how you might use it.
- You may have prepared a colour palette to guide your thinking.
- Look at different colourways before making a final choice. A paint software package on the computer is a quick way to do this.
- Think about the colours. Are they going to be fashionable and follow the season's trend? Experiment. Try different colourways.
- Evaluate your colour choice. Ask others what they think. Do the colours reflect your theme? Are they fashionable and will they sell well?

■ Decoration

- Look at your ideas for the pattern and decoration you have put on your product.
- You have worked on the style and shape, so now it is time to rearrange and perfect the decorative pattern.
- Have another look at your mood board and find new ideas; try something different! Check that the overall composition looks good.
- When you have decided on the decorative work you will need to choose the best practical techniques for doing it.
- Carry out some investigative work and produce small samples to see if the technique works for your design and on the fabrics you are likely to use.
- Evaluate each technique, explaining what the process has involved, what the results are like and if it is a technique you will use.

A *Making full use of the mood board*

Objectives

Understand how to make the right decisions about colour choice.

Understand how to use the mood board.

Understand how to develop the decorative work.

∞ links

See How designers get inspiration, pages 56–57 for more examples of moodboards.

AQA Examiner's comment

Andrew has made excellent use of his mood board by choosing interesting shapes and then using them to create a repeat pattern. This could be used as a block print when he comes to produce the lining for the bag. He also uses the board to help choose a colour palette. Designers are guided by trend forecasts. Colour is one of the most important aspects of the design. Get it wrong and your product will not sell.

AC5 communication

- Excellent layout of the images, sketched motif ideas and the repeat pattern design.
- The composition of the sheet is stunning and gives the inspiration needed for the next design stage.

Andrew is designing and making a fashion bag for the 18–35-year-old female target group (see Student exemplar **A**). The bag will form part of a summer range inspired by the theme of flowers. You will have looked at his mood board on page 140.

Frances is designing and making an educational wall hanging suitable for hanging in a child's bedroom.

B *Investigating colouring and decorative techniques for a calico wall hanging*

Abi is designing and making a sleeveless dress with a highly decorated bodice top. The decoration at the front of this low-cut dress is the main focus of this design for the 18–35-year-old female target group.

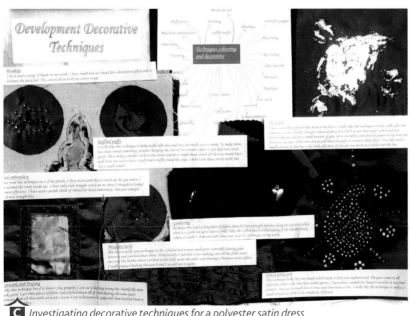

C *Investigating decorative techniques for a polyester satin dress*

AQA Examiner's comment

Frances has explored a very wide range of techniques that she believes might be useful when making up her wall hanging design. The sheet is packed with overlapping samples. She is very focused and keen to explore and evaluate techniques that will give the best effects.

AC5 communication

- The sheet is very full with overlapping pieces of work. This is acceptable, particularly when the information is analysed at a later stage.
- The evaluations of the techniques communicate their usefulness on the wall hanging.

AQA Examiner's comment

Abi has investigated a wide range of decorative techniques worked on the fabric most likely to be the one used in the final garment. Inspiration has come from India and this has been used as she works the samples. Annotation shows why she has chosen to explore the technique and if it will be of use during the making up of the garment.

AC5 communication

- The samples produced show the student's investigative and practical skills.
- The evaluative comments are good and make use of technical language.

Summary

You should now be able to:

use your mood board

decide on the best colours to use

explore different methods of decorating fabric.

How to decide on the best fabric and components

You must now choose the most suitable fabrics and components for your product. You will have to carry out some further research so you can make informed decisions.

- Choose fabrics. It is a good idea to list all the things the fabric must be if it is going to be suitable for your product, e.g. non-stretchy, washable. If you're not sure about a fabric's properties you may have to test it.

- Choose the components, including threads and fastenings. See what is in the shops, test things out and make sure they give the right effect and do their job.

- Costing – when you have considered your choice of fabrics and components you will need to do a cost chart to see if your idea is feasible. It is a good idea to seek public opinion.

- Sustainability and other environmental, moral and social issues need to be considered when you are choosing fabrics and components.

- Think about the aftercare needed and, if you have time, the design of a care label.

Zoë is designing and making an evening dress for the 18–35-year-old female target group. The dress will form part of a summer range inspired by the sea and the movement of the waves.

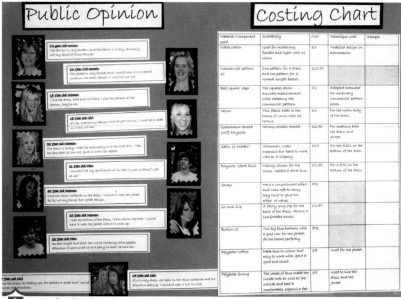

A Zoë's feedback and costing chart

Objectives

Understand how to choose the right fabrics.

Understand how to choose the right components.

Understand how to cost the product.

⬮⬮links

See Chapter 1, Fibres and Fabrics, Chapter 2, Choice of fabric and Chapter 3, Components.

 AQA Examiner's comment

Zoe has presented all of her development work to the public and asked for feedback. This will help her to make the final decisions. The costs of the fabrics and components she has chosen have been put in a chart and she has commented on their suitability. It is not necessary for students to buy very expensive fabrics as they should remember that it is the skill they show that is being marked.

AC5 communication

- Public opinion is communicated well, though a summary of findings has not been given.

- The costing chart is a good way to present this information, though a total should have been given.

- The student has not shown any samples or communicated any decision making.

Anna is designing and making a cushion for students at university, living away from home in rented accommodation.

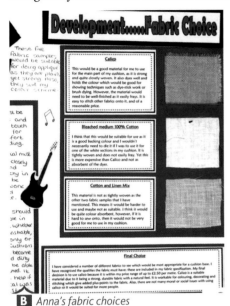

B Anna's fabric choices

Gemma is planning to make a wall hanging that will be influenced by the vibrant colours and images of Hawaii.

C Gemma's fabric choices

AQA Examiner's comment

From her own knowledge of fabrics Gemma, like Anna, has decided to choose calico but wanting to be sure of her choice she has carried out further research into the fabric. Not all of it is relevant, such as the history of calico, and this should not have been included. Time would have been better spent looking at sustainability and other environmental issues of cotton production. More useful were the samples of dyed fabric and looking at products that have been made using calico. Students must remember it does not matter when and where they carry out research on their projects as long as it is feeding them valuable information.

AC5 communication

- Excellent communication of further research carried out and decisions made.
- Excellent and appropriate use of the computer.
- Good, concise comments using technical language.

AQA Examiner's comment

Anna is an able student who has asked herself, 'What does the fabric for this cushion have to be in order to do its job well?' She has identified the properties the fabric must have. Following some research she identifies three possible fabrics and evaluates them against her properties criteria. She explains why she has chosen the calico and then presents the fabric specification for bleached medium-weight calico. She has considered the fabrics she will need for the appliqué work and has presented a range of samples. Anna also considered her choice of components, namely the fastening, thread, interfacing and beads; this is shown on her other development sheets.

AC5 communication

- There is a lot of information on this sheet, but not all of it is relevant.
- Some of the comments on the mind map show a slight lack of understanding of properties.
- Presentation is attractive and purposeful.

Summary

You should now be able to:

choose and evaluate fabrics and components

choose fabrics with fitness for purpose in mind.

11 Making

11.1 The level of demand

■ Making skills shown in the portfolio

Making the product you have designed is the most exciting and fulfilling part of one project. Remember, you are given credit for any making skills you may have shown when you were developing the product, for example:

- development of paper pattern, mock-ups, models and toiles
- samples of surface decoration and construction techniques
- samples showing the use of components including fastenings
- samples of finishing-off techniques such as bindings or overlocked edges.

The level of demand issue

It is very important that you understand what the examination board means by level of demand. They want you to produce a product that is sufficiently complex but also very well made to gain the highest marks. Compare the products shown on these pages.

Product shape and style

- How demanding will they be to make?
- Are they complex or very basic?
- How much thought and preparation do they require?
- How many special features are there?
- How much work is involved and how long would it take to make?

Fabrics and components

- Have a range of fabrics and components been used?
- How difficult are the fabrics to handle?
- Do they fray easily?
- How difficult are they to sew?
- Do the edges need special finishing?
- Do they slip or pucker easily when being stitched?
- Do they crease badly and need careful handling?

Construction techniques involved

- How many different techniques are involved in the construction of the product?
- How demanding and how much of a challenge is the construction?
- Does it involve parts made on a subassembly production line?
- Are there any demanding special features?

Colouring or decorative techniques involved

- Has the background colour been applied by the student or has bought fabric been used?
- Are the decorative parts worked by hand or machine, or are they bought motifs?
- How many different techniques have been used?
- Are they difficult, challenging or time consuming?
- What will be the quality of the finished look?

AQA Examiner's comment

This is a complex, very well-made wall hanging that involves many techniques. All the fabrics have been designed and coloured by the student. The shaped edges, the pocket with button and buttonholes, the appliqué work, the tabs and the hand stitching are done well and, though the painted word 'Africa' is poor, there is still enough evidence for the student to gain a high mark. In order to make it in the time allowed the student must have been very well prepared and have worked quickly and efficiently.

A *Wall hanging inspired by the theme of Africa*

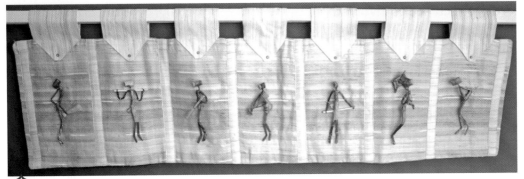

 B *Wall hanging inspired by the people of Africa*

 C *Fashion top*

 Cotton gingham children's dress

This summer dress has been made using a commercial pattern so it has involved very little development of the design. The marks awarded for designing are likely to be low. The dress is a basic design and relatively easy to make when you follow the pattern instructions. The white braid and beads have been hand stitched into place and the finished dress looks very attractive. The student will not achieve the highest marks because there is little complex skill shown in either the construction or the decorative work.

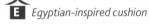 Egyptian-inspired cushion

This small, though very well-made, cushion is complex in its structure and is made out of silky fabrics, which are difficult to handle. The shape is complex to make accurately and the stitching is done well. The back of the cushion is decorated and there is a button and buttonhole opening. The work is original and shows high levels of accuracy and finish. This product is likely to achieve a high mark.

Summary

You should now be able to:

understand what is meant by level of demand and modify your product accordingly.

11.2 Evidence in folders

■ Presenting the final design and planning for making

Remember, a third party should be able to make your design from the information you present. Depending on how much time you have, you may decide to put all the information on one sheet and present it as a manufacturing specification or you might prefer to produce:

- a coloured presentation drawing of the final design
- a working or technical drawing
- manufacturing production plans – e.g. flow diagrams, Gantt charts
- production records, including photographs you took as you made the product.

Presentation boards

In industry designers will have to sell their ideas and one way of doing this is to impress the client with presentation boards illustrating the product, in full colour and showing off the products best features.

Working or technical drawings

These are usually detailed drawings often done to scale with full details of measurements and sizes. Front and back views and sometimes exploded diagrams of special features are included. Using black fine-line pen and clear, smooth lines gives the best effect.

Production plans

It is often difficult to plan out the stages of making your product because of your lack of experience. From the modelling you have done you should be able to produce a simple plan to show how you will make the product. Some students use flow diagrams and others prefer Gantt charts.

Production records

As you make your product it is useful to keep careful records. Presenting the information in chart form is often the quickest way. Include photographs if possible. Doing this is helpful when you come to:

- evaluate your work
- write the manufacturing specification
- suggest modifications for mass manufacture.

Manufacturing specification

This is the final specification, which provides everyone in the factory working on the manufacture with all the details about the product. It ensures that they all work to the same plan using the same materials, components, measurements and techniques. It is a quality assurance measure.

Objectives

Learn about the evidence you have to show to meet the assessment criteria for making.

links

See Chapter 7 Production planning.

Sarah is designing and making an evening dress inspired by the insect world.

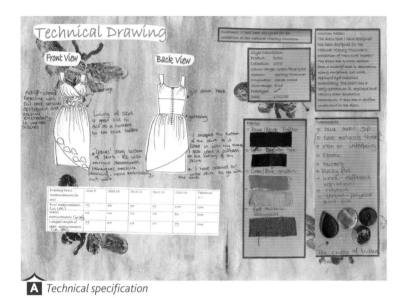

 Technical specification

AC5 communication

- There is excellent detail about the manufacturing criteria.
- Using a coloured background to the text often makes it difficult to read.

AQA Examiner's comment

Sarah is making a sleeveless evening dress, which is quite a challenge considering the amount of decorative work she intends to incorporate. This design sheet gives details for manufacturing the garment from the working drawing to fabric choice and details of components. From all the detail provided in her portfolio a third party should be able to make up her design.

Katie is designing and making a wall hanging inspired by African culture.

Production Plan

Date. Time Taken (hours)	Work Carried Out?	Modifications. How have you altered this stage from your original plans?	How would this be carried out in industry?	Quality control checks.	Risk assessment. Health and safety issues.
3/12/07 (2 hours)	Produced a paper pattern and bought fabrics and components.	Altered size of pattern pieces and found a bigger range of fabrics than originally thought.	The production manager would order fabrics & components. Paper pattern cut out on PC CAD.	Fabrics checked for faults and dirty marks. Components checked for faults. Fabrics specification checked	Risks of fabric rolls falling on them whilst handling them.
11/12/07 (2 hours)	Cut out each piece and dyed main panel background.	Changed the area in which coloured on main panel.	Dyed all in one go then cut out.	Make sure all is evenly dyed. Toxic dyes and fumes checked.	No toxins given off. waste may enter sewage works
17/12/07 (1 hour)	Pressed main piece, arranged each piece in formation and then began dye stick panel.	The main piece I had left to be bigger then originally planned. Also left out one panel due to how much time I had to work with which changed original arrangement of wall hanging	Cut by a specific sizing machine.	Standard check before making.	Iron may burn workers or fabric.
14/01/08 (3 hours)	Completed dye stick panel and decided to add cut work to it.	Added cut-work to the dye stick panel to add more interest and make the product more eye-catching. Also I changed some original placing of colours.	Done with a laser cutter. Hand work panel possibly produced in a developing country and bought in as a component.	Check all stitching is in tacked. Checked for accuracy and colouring checked.	Risk of toxic dyes, laser cutter may hard worker if they were in the way.

 A section of Katie's wall hanging production records

AC5 communication

- Neat, well-written diary giving a clear explanation of the work involved.
- It is useful to record the time taken for each process.

AQA Examiner's comment

Katie has kept ongoing records as she has made the wall hanging. All the information recorded here will be useful when she comes to evaluate the hanging, write the manufacturing specification and make suggestions for modifications. She is also meeting the assessment criteria by planning her time, showing an awareness of industrial processes, addressing quality control and highlighting health and safety issues.

Summary

You should now be able to:

successfully present your final design.

11.3 Making skills

Assessing your making skills

Throughout your project your teacher will be monitoring your performance. Your assessment is not just based on the finished outcome; it is also based on your working methods. In order to gain the highest marks you will need to remember the following:

- The product must be demanding and show high levels of skill.
- Handling fabrics and techniques must present a challenge.
- Be an independent worker.
- Work with speed and efficiency, care and accuracy.
- Choose the correct tools, materials, components, equipment and techniques.
- Show quality finish at every stage.
- Use the modern technology available to you – sublimation printers, computerised sewing machines, scanner cutters for stencils, milling machines for printing blocks.
- Adopt safe working practices.
- Apply quality controls and risk assessments.
- Correct working errors and modify your work as you go along.
- Develop a system for recording and justifying the changes you make.
- The product must be high quality and suitable for the target market.
- Suggest modifications to make the product suitable for mass production.
- Support your making evidence with photographs.

Textile products

When you look through this chapter you will get lots of ideas for products you might make. Take care not to be too ambitious but also be careful not to make a product that is too simple. Ties, sarongs and scarves may be fashionable but they show very few construction skills. Here are some examples of textile products:

- children – fashion garments, sleepwear, educational, products for bedrooms
- fashion garments – skirts, trousers, fashion tops, lingerie, swimwear
- accessories – bags, hats
- pets – sleeping products, garments, toys
- interiors – wall hangings, cushions, 3D sculptures, picture frames, table wear
- carrying containers – bags, holdalls, rucksacks, boxes.

Controlled assessment tasks

Innovative and unique children's learning toys are very popular as gifts. An exclusive craft shop has commissioned you to produce a range of original designs that will appeal to their customers. Design and make a textile product that will be an educational toy for the 0–5-year-age range.

A *Fabric book*

A manufacturing company, which supplies gift shops around the British Isles, has commissioned you to design a range of textiles: decorative products inspired by a specific theme such as sea-life centres, animal farms and flowers. Design and make one of the products from the range that would be a best-seller with the visitors.

AQA Examiner's comment This is a suitable product to design and make for this controlled task. It has given the student ample opportunity to show her skills. The book has made excellent use of the modern technology available and the result is a very marketable product.

B *Fish cushion*

AQA Examiner's comment The student has designed and made a very creative cushion inspired by fishes. However, even though the shape is challenging and the overall effect appealing, the work lacks quality and standard of finish.

Summary

You should now be able to:

make your product showing the necessary skills

choose suitable products to make

make products for children.

Making textile products

Examples of textile products

A popular high street store has commissioned you to design a fashion garment or accessory to wear at a special occasion event. Your design is to be inspired by the colours, spirit, patterns and shapes of an identified festival, such as Chinese New Year, the Dragon Boat Race, Glastonbury, Holi (Festival of Colours), the Rio carnival.

AQA Examiner's comment
This clutch bag has been inspired by carnival, which is reflected well in the colour and fabric choices. The bag is a simple style but is very effective. It is fully lined and has an inserted zip-fastened pocket. The bag is very attractive and was made within the time limit.

A *Celebration-inspired fashion bag*

You have been commissioned by a national supermarket chain to design a range of smart casual wear for the 18+ year age range. The client is keen to promote the current trend forecast. Design a range for the autumn collection and make up a prototype of one product.

AQA Examiner's comment
Waistcoats and fashion tops are a good choice of product as they can be decorated easily and alsao show some complex making skills. This waistcoat is very attractive and reflects the theme well. Modern appliqué techniques have been used and there is a high standard of accuracy and finish.

B *Autumn-leaf-inspired waistcoat*

Design and make a promotional fashion garment or accessory for the window display of a high street Oxfam shop; it should be made from recycled donated textiles.

Examiner's comment
This first example of a cushion is a good choice of product as it makes excellent use of recycled fabrics and components. It is very modern, attractive and very achievable in the time available. The stitching is attractive and gives a very effective look.

C *Cushion made from recycled textiles*

Examiner's comment
This second example of bags have been made by the same student who was exploring the use of reclaimed garments from a charity shop. The denim bag has been made from a pair of jeans and is made to look vintage style with tucks, lettering and appliqué. The second bag is made from a woollen coat, a gathered summer skirt and a curtain.
The beads and flower accessories were also reclaimed. Both bags are very well made and meet the requirements of the task well. Most candidates would be unlikely to have the time to make both bags and should restrict themselves to one.

Summary

You should now be able to:

choose suitable products to make in response to the tasks set

make attractive products using recycled garments.

D *Two bags made from recycled textile garments*

▪ Controlled assessment tasks

You have been asked by a national art gallery to design a range of fashion accessories or home interior products inspired by the work of a featuring artist e.g. Gustav Klimt. Make up one item from your range that will appeal to the gallery's gift shop visitors.

A *Fruit-inspired fashion bag*

AQA Examiner's comment Students exemplar A and B show how two different students have responded to the task set. Both have been inspired by famous artists who have painted fruit in 'still life', but the decorative products they have made are very different. A wide range of decorative skills have been used, including screen printing, cut work, embroidery and quilting. The standard of accuracy and finish is excellent and both products would have achieved high marks.

B *Fruit-inspired wall hanging*

Many young people are keen to go to university. Student accommodation is often very basic and without the home comforts many are used to. A charity shop on a university campus has invited you to design a range of textile products that would prove popular with students. Make at least one product that could be sold at the university shop.

C *Chocolate and marshmallow wall hanging*

AQA Examiner's comment

This delicious-looking wall hanging has been inspired by chocolate and marshmallow. As well as using fabric printed by the student it makes full use of recycled fabrics. It has been designed for the teenage market and would be achievable in the time allowed.

A manufacturing company that supplies gift shops around the British Isles has commissioned you to design a range of textiles and decorative products inspired by a specific theme such as sea life centres, animal farms or flowers. Design and make one of the products from the range that would be a bestseller with the visitors.

AQA Examiner's comment

This very simple but effective cushion would be a very marketable product in a gift shop. The design is modern, suitable for mass production and this prototype could be made well within the time limit. The cushion pad is held within the cushion by a flap, held in place by press studs. The final product does not show a full range of challenging skills but there was a lot of evidence in the development section of the folder to show that other techniques had been trialled and tested.

D *Flower-inspired cushion*

Summary

You will be able to:

make your product showing the necessary skills

choose suitable products for the task you have chosen

understand the level of accuracy and finish needed.

Evidence of using modern technology in your work

Computers are used at every stage in product design and manufacture and benefit those working in the textile industry.

As a designer you should use all modern technologies available to you. If you are lucky enough to have up-to-date equipment in your school and it offers you the best way of carrying out the task then use it:

- to help with research
- during the development of your design
- to aid manufacturing
- to help during testing and evaluating.

Throughout the book, you will see examples of how modern technology has been used.

Objectives

Learn about using modern technology to benefit your coursework.

⊙⊙links

See Chapter 8 ICT.

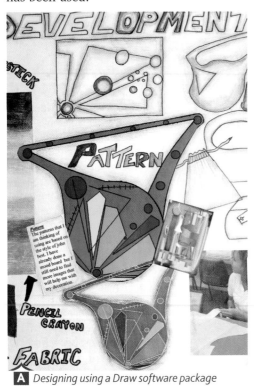

A Designing using a Draw software package

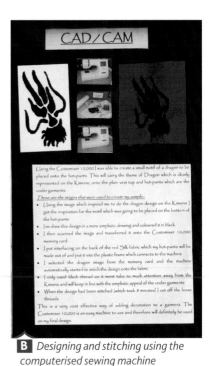

B Designing and stitching using the computerised sewing machine

Controlled assessment tasks

A school uniform designer has recognised a gap in the market for outdoor school uniform products such as a bag, jacket, hat and scarf that offer a child protection in the dark. Design and make a 'Sew and be Seen' school uniform product for young children that incorporates reflective 'glow in the dark' fabrics and a special sound or light feature.

Sandra is designing and making a school bag for young teenagers. She has incorporated the use of modern technology and included a fluorescent element so the bag is visible in the dark.

This is a suitable product to design and make for this task though marks awarded would have been higher had she incorporated the light or sound feature. However the bag is complex in its design and has given the student ample opportunity to show her skills. She has used modern technology with the sublimation printer and the computerised sewing machine. This is a very well-made product.

C *School bag*

Many young people are keen to go to university. Student accommodation is often very basic and without the home comforts many are used to. A student charity shop on a university campus has invited you to design a range of textile products that would prove popular with students. Make at least one decorative product that could be sold at the university shop.

Shirain has made a very simple cushion using recycled fabrics. To make the product personal she has included a photograph printed on the sublimation printer.

This is an attractive cushion and is well made using recycled fabrics. Unfortunately it does not have sufficient technical skill to be awarded the highest marks.

D *Cushion*

Using technology to communicate your coursework to the examination board

e-Portfolios

Some schools are very well equipped with cameras and ICT facilities and teachers encourage students to submit their work on a CD-R or send it directly to the examination board by e-Portfolio. Either of these methods allows you to use video clips, which can be an excellent way to communicate information, particularly how well your finished product works.

Summary

You should now be able to:

know when to use the modern technology available in your school

understand how ICT can enhance your work.

12 Testing and evaluation

12.1 Testing and evaluating throughout the task

■ Testing and evaluating throughout the process

In order to design and make a textile product that meets the requirements of the design brief and will sell well to the public, you have to keep checking that your ideas will work. All aspects must be of the highest quality so you must evaluate and improve at every stage. There are a number of ways you will be expected to do this:

- Evaluate and use your initial research.
- Evaluate your design ideas against the specifications.
- Show your ideas to the intended users to collect feedback comments.
- Seek expert opinions.
- Test and evaluate the appropriateness of materials, components, techniques and processes.
- Test, trial and evaluate through sampling and prototyping.
- Compare your own product design to a similar existing one.
- Carry out a full product analysis on your made outcome.

Evaluation during the research process

You will carry out research during various stages of the task. Initially you will look for information that is going to inspire and inform before you start presenting your ideas. You are likely to:

- collect material from a wide range of sources and evaluate its usefulness before you decide to present it in your folder
- evaluate the images on the mood board and perhaps use them to test if they are suitable for creating colour schemes, patterns, shapes and textures
- study and evaluate key features found on existing designs.

Evaluating existing products

You will need to examine and evaluate how other designers have:

- shaped and styled their products
- used colour
- chosen fabrics and components
- used decorative techniques
- constructed the product
- decided on size and special features
- labelled, priced and packaged.

You can do this through observation during shop visits, looking at photographs and disassembling an actual product. It is sensible to

Objectives

Understand the testing and evaluating methods appropriate to every stage.

Learn how to evaluate your research.

∞links

See Testing and evaluating design ideas, pages 68–69.

record your evaluations by the side of each existing design and then make a statement summarising your findings.

Kim has designed a wall hanging to promote the 'Save Our Rainforest' campaign.

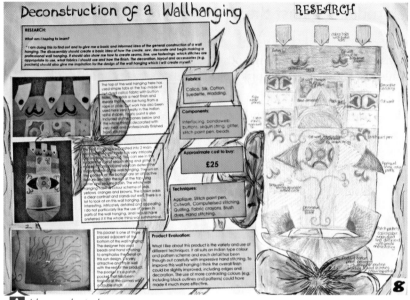

  Ideas evaluated

Natalie has also made a wall hanging inspired by the rain forest. She recognises that her design is a one-off but the task asks her to consider mass production.

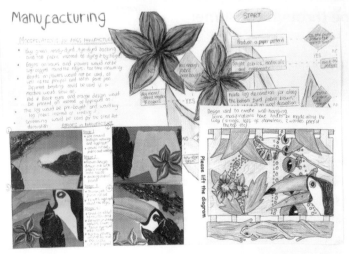

B *Modifying the design idea*

AQA Examiner's comment Natalie has photographed the stages she went through when making the hanging. She has used this information to help her produce a flow diagram which illustrates the main stages in the making process. She has suggested modifications in a bullet-pointed list. As she made the hanging she evaluated its success and could see improvements for a new design. The improved modified design is also presented.

 links

See Product disassembly, pages 62–63.

AQA Examiner's comment Kim has presented two coloured ideas for the wall hanging. They have been evaluated against the design specification and a concise evaluation has been presented. A quick and effective way of evaluating designs is to produce a star profile. Kim has chosen the six main criteria from the specification to make up the profile and given each a mark out of six. You can spot weaknesses very quickly.

AC5 communication

- Designs have been watercoloured showing an alternative technique to coloured pencils.
- Back view and exploded diagrams are useful.
- The text is difficult to read – a larger font size should be used.

AC5 communication

- This is a very informative design sheet with decisions presented in a clear and coherent manner.
- Photographs are useful.
- Flow diagrams are a good way to communicate the making process.

Summary

You should now be able to:

identify when and where you need to test and evaluate

evaluate existing designs.

12.2 Using specifications and consumers to test and evaluate

■ Testing and evaluating the product against the specifications

Specifications are needed at various stages through the designing and making of a textile product. The main ones used during textile product manufacture are as follows:

- fabric specifications – characteristics, properties, quality and cost
- design specifications – the function, target market, performance, safety and quality, design, appearance, theme, budget, social, moral, ethical or environmental issues, shape and style, lifecycle, packaging, sustainability
- product specifications that describe in detail every aspect of the prototype or final product – photo/working drawing, fabric and components, stitching and techniques information, size/measurements, care label and costing
- manufacturing specifications – details given to a third party to make the product in quantity.

You must decide on the best way to test and evaluate whether your product meets the criteria set out in these specifications.

When you have made your product it is a good idea to use a chart to record your testing.

■ Testing the product prototype through consumer trials

As a designer you need to check with the user, experts and retailers that they think the product:

- is fit for purpose
- is good value for money
- is a stylish design, has appeal and they like it
- has a suitable choice of materials, components and techniques
- will be easy to maintain and look after
- will be safe to use and will not harm the environment.

The views of intended users can be collected by asking a sample of the target market to try out the product and record their opinions on how well it performed. The following methods could be used:

- questionnaire
- interview
- photographs or videos taken.

Heidi has designed and made an educational product for young children. It is a giant giraffe, which holds small toys in alphabet pockets.

∞ links

See Manufacturing specifications, pages 110–111.

A *Record of testing*

Specification criteria	The bag will hold small personal items
Test	Place the items in your made bag
Result/Findings	The weight of the items caused the bag to sag slightly
Modification	A stronger, less stretchy fabric will need to be used for the bag

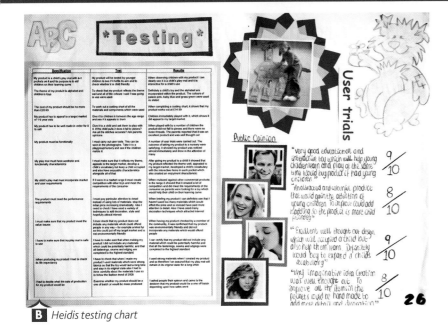

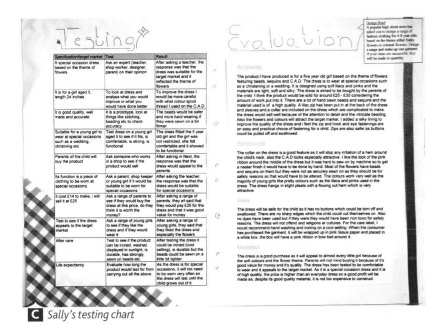

B *Heidis testing chart*

AQA Examiner's comment

Heidi has produced a chart to help her focus on evaluating the toy against the criteria set out in the specifications. Though the chart headings are inaccurate she has outlined the need for testing and how the product has performed. The photograph shows a child using the product and many of her evaluative comments come from observing the child at play. Heidi has also asked a sample of the public their opinion. They have given her some useful suggestions for improvements and a mark out of 10.

Sally has designed and made a dress for 4–8-year-olds based on the theme of 'funky flowers'.

AQA Examiner's comment

Sally has produced a chart which lists the main specification criteria, suggests a testing strategy and then presents the results. Her findings are then written up into a product analysis report. It would have been a good idea for Sally to suggest modifications to the design.

C *Sally's testing chart*

Final evaluation product analysis reports

■ Comparing your product with a similar commercial product

It is a useful exercise to compare your product with a similar commercial one. Take photographs and describe both products. You might want to present your findings in chart form. Observations could include your opinion, sales figures, whether it is fashionable, the cost and aftercare needed.

■ Writing the final evaluation report

Your prototype has been put through a rigorous testing and evaluating process. You will have collected information through:

- testing and evaluating against the specifications
- seeking opinions of users, retailer and other experts
- testing and evaluating the materials, components, techniques and processes
- comparing your own product design with a similar existing one.

To meet the assessment criteria you must now pull all this information together, carry out a full product analysis and present your findings in a final report that could be used by a potential manufacturer.

Some points to help you

As you write the report ask yourself the following questions:

- Will the end user be satisfied with the product?
- Is it a safe product to manufacture and also to use?
- Will it work as you intended?
- Is it modern, fashionable, with appealing aesthetics?
- Will it sell for the correct price and will it be value for money?
- Is it made to agreed standards? You may want to highlight tolerance levels.
- Are the materials and techniques appropriate and do they work well?
- Does the product have a low impact on the environment?
- Can it be modified to make it suitable for mass production?

For each of these you need to make full comments and explain your final decisions.

Objectives

Learn how you can compare your product with a similar commercial one.

Learn how to write final evaluation reports.

Understand evaluating and justifying the need for modifications to the product.

Abi has designed and made a strapless, sleeveless dress for the teenage market. The design has been presented on the catwalk at a local fashion show.

 Seeking public opinion

> **AQA Examiner's comment**
>
> Having your design modelled and presented on the catwalk is a good way to gauge public opinion and to find out what the target market thinks of your work. It is a good idea to put a short questionnaire on the audience's seats. Abi has also compared her design with a similar product bought from Monsoon. Her evaluation would have been improved by making a summary statement showing which offered best value for money.

Kelly has made a fruit-inspired wall hanging for decorating the walls of an ice-cream parlour. She recognises that her design is a prototype and has produced an extensive report to an industrial manufacturer.

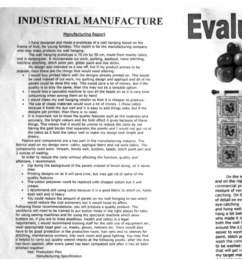

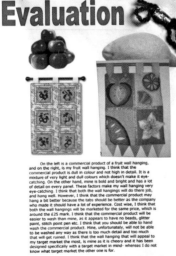

 Evaluating the wall hanging

> **AQA Examiner's comment**
>
> Kelly has written a full report to the manufacturer suggesting alterations to the design, the choice of fabrics and components and methods of manufacture. In addition she has given some advice about health and safety issues in the workplace. When students refer to industrial practices they need to make sure it is in direct reference to their product.

AC5 communication

- The written comments lack some depth of thinking.
- The photographs of the fashion show are very effective.
- The questionnaire would have been of more value if the information had been used and a conclusion drawn.

AC5 communication

- A neat, well-presented page. The written piece is presented in a report format that makes the information very accessible.
- The evaluation comparing the two products is concise and fluent though a chart may have been a better way of doing a direct comparison.

Summary

You should now be able to:

compare your design with a commercial product

write a final product evaluation report.

Glossary

A

Aesthetics: the visual design appeal.

Annotation: written labels and notes.

Automatic: operation carried out by machine, to assist an operator (semi-automatic) or to complete the task independently (fully automatic).

B

Bias binding: a fabric strip cut diagonally across fabric. The long edges are folded under and the strip is folded in half along its length. This is the binding strip that can be used to cover the raw edge of other fabrics.

Biodegradable: can be broken down naturally through the action of bacteria or other living organisms.

Blended fibre: two or more fibres spun together to make a yarn.

Bonded: webs of fibres are pressed together using adhesives or heat.

C

CAD: computer-aided design.

CAM: computer-aided manufacture.

Care label: contains information on how to care for and maintain a product.

Client: the person or company that employs the designer to design a product.

Closed-loop process: manufacturing process whereby all waste is reused in the production system.

Colourfast: how well a fabric keeps dyes applied to it, even through regular washing.

Colour palette: also colourway; the colour or range of colours selected for the design of fabric or product.

Comparative shop: research activity to compare and contrast two or more similar existing products; results may be presented as a report or in a table.

Concealed fastening: fastening that cannot be seen on the outside of the product. It can be hidden in a seam or by a flap of fabric.

Costume designer: creator of clothing for actors to wear during filming or theatre productions. Design specifications will include set and stage requirements related to lighting effects, quick changes between scenes, and perhaps a series of the same costume for different parts of the drama.

Critical control points (CCPs): the stages at which checks are made.

Customising: taking previously made pieces and transforming them into new designs by restyling or adding embellishments. Also known as **upcycling**.

D

Disassembly: examining closely, unpicking seams and taking apart to reduce the product to its cut-out pieces of fabric and components.

Distressed: the way a fabric has been damaged/changed from its original state to give texture, colour or an aged look.

Drape: how a fabric hangs.

Drawstring: a type of fastening; also a way to reduce fullness in a product.

E

Eco-label: found on an environmentally friendly product; awarded because of content or manufacturing system.

Embossing: a relief print pressed into a fabric, changing its surface texture as well as giving a patterned appearance.

Ethical: according to moral values.

F

Fabric: a sheet or length of cloth made from fibres or yarns.

Fabric specification: a list of requirements for a fabric, written down to help in the selection of the fabric.

Facing: fabric is cut to the same pattern as the main fabric. The facing and main fabrics are placed right sides together, stitched around leaving a gap in the stitching, and then turned through. This results in a neat finished edge. For example, facing is used for sleeveless dress bodices.

Fair trade: a partnership between producers and consumers that ensures the workers receive a fair wage, better access to markets in developed countries and community support.

Fast fashion: fashionable clothing trend moving from catwalk to high street in record time; brief interest soon replaced by next fashion update.

Felted: fibres are pressed together using heat, moisture and agitation, or hot needles.

Fibre: a hair-like structure that is the basis of a yarn or fabric.

Filament: a long fibre that can be used alone or twisted with others to make smooth yarn.

Flammability: liability to catch fire.

Fusible: can stick to a fabric, using heat to fuse.

G

Green fibre: an alternative sustainable source of fibre for a yarn or fabric.

H

Handle: what a fabric is like to hold and work with.

Haute couture: the French term for the highest quality designer garments.

Hazard: a step or process that could cause harm or injury.

Hypoallergenic: unlikely to cause an allergic reaction.

I

Indirect costs: business expenses not directly attributable to any particular product, also known as overheads.

Insulate: add warmth to a fabric to keep heat regulated.

Interactive fabrics: a product that requires a power source to activate its features.

Interfacing: an extra layer of material between the main fabric and the lining fabric.

Interlining: light bonded fabric that often has dry glue on one side. It can be ironed on to the reverse side of the main fabric to strengthen it. When the dry glue is heated it bonds the two layers together.

J

Jacquard: a complex weave or a loom for complex weaves.

L

Laminated: two or more fabrics bonded together to enhance the fabric's properties.

Landfill: where waste is dumped and then covered over.

Legislation: laws.

M

Manikin: also mannequin or dressmakers' dummy in a human-shaped form, for designing and testing garments.

Manipulated: moving fabric by hand to shape and position folds, or when a fabric is moved, folded, stretched or handled to change its look, fit and texture.

Manufacturing specification: describes the stages of manufacture and materials needed in order to make the product.

Micro-encapsulation: substances that are fixed to the fabric or the fibre and can then be activated, such as perfumes.

Microfibre: a synthetic fibre that is made 60 times finer than a human hair.

Mind map: also brainstorm or thought shower: a chart/diagram listing thoughts/ideas as they occur. Words may be linked by arrows to show the thought process.

Mixed fibre: two or more yarns mixed together in the construction of the fabric.

Mordant: a chemical used to fix a dye to fibres and fabrics.

N

Natural fibre: a fibre that comes from a plant or animal source.

O

Organic: produced using natural fertilisers, pesticides and herbicides to protect the biodiversity of the environment and workers' health.

Overheads: factory running costs – electricity for machinery, heating, lighting, water rates, building rent, administration costs, etc.

Overlocking: a method of neatening seams in industry using a machine with three or more threads to trim, stitch and edge-finish the seam.

P

Pattern master: a ruler with straight edges and curved edges to make drawing paper patterns easier.

Pigment: a colour used to dye fibres and fabrics, which can come from a natural or synthetic source.

Pile weave: loops or cut loops form a raised texture on the fabric.

Pinking shears: cut a zigzag edge, which helps to prevent woven fabrics from fraying.

Placket: the strip down the front opening of a shirt in which the buttonholes are stitched.

Plain weave: a simple basic weave with alternating yarns between weft and warp.

Polymerisation: the process by which monomers are joined together to form polymers.

Pre-manufactured: made ready to use in a factory.

Product specification: describes the prototype or final product. It includes photo/working drawing, fabric and components, stitching and techniques information, size/measurements, care label and costing.

Prototype: the first trial product made to test materials, techniques and processes.

PVC: polyvinyl chloride.

Q

Quality assurance: the guarantee that the product is a quality product.

Quality control (QC): products are checked to assess whether they conform to set standards.

Quality label: given to a product that has passed a standards test for the quality of the item or the system by which it has been produced.

R

Recycled: a product that has been reused in some form.

Regenerated fibre: natural cellulose treated with artificial chemicals to extract the fibres.

Relief: relief printing and dyeing means something is used to block the dyes from absorbing and is called a relief, e.g. string on tie dye or card on stencilling.

Renewable energy: electricity generated from sources that will not be depleted, such as from wind and solar power.

Resources: materials, people and machinery involved in making the product.

S

Safety label: shows the product has passed safety testing standards.

Satin weave: the weft or the warp goes over four or more yarns, giving a high, smooth sheen to the fabric.

Search engine: an internet tool to list web pages that feature the word or words entered in the search box.

Sharps: standard, long hand-sewing needles, or a term used in industry to refer to pins and needles in general.

Slow clothes: fashionable clothing that is bought, used and worn into the ground before discarding.

Smart fabrics: a textile product that changes owing to its environment, without human intervention.

Spray diffuser: a hinged metal tube used to blow dye or ink on to fabric or paper.

Spreadsheet: a table of data, which can be used to store information. Use Microsoft Excel to create spreadsheets and calculate data.

Squeegee: a tool with a rubber blade, used to spread print paste across a screen.

Staple: a short fibre that needs to be twisted with others to make a yarn.

Sustainable: can be manufactured with little or no negative impact on the environment and on the health and wellbeing of the workers employed to make the product.

Synthetic fibre: entirely artificial and made using oil and coal in its chemical production.

System: the method of putting together the individual parts.

T

Tally chart: a system to record the number of times something occurs; tallies are usually grouped into fives for speed of counting.

Target market: target group; the intended user/buyer.

Task analysis: working out what needs to be done in order to respond to the design brief.

Technique: a method used to add a feature to a fabric.

Toile: a model of a garment, often made from inexpensive cotton calico.

Trade name: a name given to a fibre created and sold by a company such as Nylon (named by Dupont) – where polyamide is its, generic name.

Twill weave: weft goes under more than one warp thread, making a diagonal stripe pattern on the fabric.

U

UV protection: will shield wearer from harmful ultra-violet radiation in sunlight.

W

Warp knit: loops linked in a vertical direction.

Wearable electronics: electronic devices that are embedded into fabric or incorporated into clothing for sensing, monitoring, communication and entertainment purposes.

Weft knit: loops linked across the width of the fabric.

Weight: of a fabric is indicated by the thickness and fibre type of the yarn and/or the denseness of the weave or knit.

Working drawings: also known as flats; line drawings of garments, drawn to scale using simple, clear lines to show seams, darts, pockets, buttons, trims, etc.

Workstations: areas laid out to enable the worker to organise resources, use correct machinery and stack completed work in the most efficient way.

Woven fabric: interlacing yarns with warp running down the length and weft running across the fabric.

Y

Yarn: a thread-like structure that is made from either short staple fibres twisted together or long filament fibres.

Index

Note: key terms are in bold

3D modelling   102–5

A

aesthetics   22
analysis
   product   60–1
   research   60–1, 138–9
annotation   62
automatic   98

B

bias binding   108, 109
biodegradable   18
blended fibres   22, 22–3
blocks   96–7
bonded   26–7, 27

C

CAD   123–7, 125
CAM   126, 126–7
care label   39
choice of fabric   34–7
   designer's role   34
client   57
closed-loop process   18
colour development   148–9
colour forecasts   56–7
colour palette   57
coloured ideas, design ideas
   142–3
colourfast   30
colouring, hand tools/equipment   94–5
comparative shop   116, 117
components
   fastenings   46–9
   future   50–1
   textile components   50–1
computers   97, 104–5, 164–5
   design   122–5
   ICT   120–7
   in manufacturing   126–7
   presentation   123
concealed fastening   46
construction techniques   106–11
consumer rights
   designing safe products   86–7
   labelling   86
consumers, testing/evaluating   168–9
controlled assessment tasks
   inspirational made outcomes   162–3
   making skills   158–9
   modern technology   164–5
costing a product   116–17
costume designer   68
critical control points (CCPs)   118, 118–19
cultural influences   72–5

customising   79
cutting, hand tools/equipment   95

D

decoration development   148–9
design
   moral issues   76–7
   sustainability   82
design brief   57
design ideas
   coloured ideas   142–3
   planning the development
      144–5
   sketched ideas   140–1
   testing/evaluating   68–9
design opportunity   134–9
   analysing the task   134–5
   design contexts   134
   research   136–9
design proposal   140–51
design specifications   139
research analysis   64
testing/evaluating   64–5
designing for a purpose   61
designing, hand tools/equipment   94–5
designing safe products, consumer rights   86–7
disassembly   62, 62–3
   pattern development from   63
   research using   62–3
distressed   45
drape   30
drawstring   49
dyeing   40–1

E

e-portfolios   165
eco-label   39
electronics, wearable electronics   72–4
embellishing, hand tools/equipment   94–5
embossing   30, 30–1
environmental issues   82–5
ethical   64
ethical fabric production   84–5
ethical issues   34, 76–7
   product costing   117
evaluating see testing/evaluating
evidence in folders, making
   156–7

F

fabric/component choice   150–1
fabric enhancement   44–5
   manipulation   44–5
   surface decoration   44
fabric finishes   30–1
fabric specification   36–7, 37
fabrics   10, 10–11
   choice of fabric   34–7

future   32–3
   names   34–5
   synthetic   14–17
facing   111
fair trade   34, 76–7
fast fashion   79
fastenings   46–9
felted   26–7, 27
fibres   10, 10–23
   future   32–3
filament   10
finishes, fabric   30–1
flammability   87
flowcharts, production   112–13
fusible   51
future
   components   50–1
   fibres/fabrics   32–3
   trend forecasts   56–7

G

green fibres   22, 22–3

H

hand tools/equipment   94–7
   see also machinery
handle   12
haute couture   101
hazard   87, 88–9
health and safety   86–9
   consumer rights   86–7
   risk assessments   88–9
heated equipment   96
hypoallergenic   87

I

ICT see computers
indirect costs   116
industrial machinery   98
inspiration   56–9
inspirational made outcomes, controlled
   assessment tasks   162–3
insulate   51
interactive fabrics   32, 32–3
interfacing   51
interlining   111

J

jacquard   24, 25
just-in-time stock control (JIT)   101

K

knitted fabrics   28–9

L

labelling   38–9
   consumer rights   86
   sustainability   82–3

laminated 26–7, 27
landfill 79
legislation 87
level of demand, making skills 152–5
Lyocell, case study 20

M

machinery 98–9
 see also hand tools/equipment
making
 evidence in folders 156–7
 methods for 110–11
 seams 106–7
 textile products 160–1
making skills 152–5, 158–9
 assessing 158
 controlled assessment tasks 158–9
 textile products 158
manikin (mannequin) 96–7, 97, 103–4
manipulated 45
manipulation, fabric enhancement 44–5
manufacturing, computers in 126–7
manufacturing specification 64, 64–5,
 114–15
marking, hand tools/equipment 95
measuring, hand tools/equipment 95
methods for making 110–11
micro-encapsulation 27
microfibres 14, 15
mind map 57
mixed fibres 22, 22–3
modelling, 3D 102–5
modern technology 164–5
 knitted fabrics 29
 non-woven fabrics 27
mood boards 58–9
moral issues 34, 76–7
mordant 40

N

names, fabric 34–5
natural fabrics 12–13
natural fibres 12, 12–13
 properties 12–13
new technology *see* modern technology
non-woven fabrics 26–7

O

organic 39
organic cotton 83, 84
overheads 116
overlocking 98

P

pattern development from disassembly 63
pattern master 95
pigment 40
pile weave 24, 25
pinking shears 95
placket 111
plain weave 24, 25
planning

design ideas 144–5
production 112–19
research 136
polymerisation 14
pre-manufactured 51
presentation, computers 123
presenting the final design 156–7
printing 42–3
product analysis 60–1
 final evaluation reports 170–1
product comparison 71
product cost comparison 117
product costing 116–17
product development techniques 102–5
product disassembly 62–3
product research, existing 60
product specification 64, 64–5, 115
production flowcharts 112–13
production planning 112–19
production systems/processes 100–1
prototypes 66, 105
PVC 27

Q

quality assurance 66, 66–7
quality control (QC) 112, 118–19
quality label 39

R

recycled 39
recycling textiles 78–81
regenerated fibres 18, 18–21
relief 42
renewable energy 82
reports, testing/evaluating 170–1
research
 analysis 60–1, 138–9
 carrying out 136–7
 design ideas 68–9
 design opportunity 136–9
 design specifications 64
 existing product research 60
 planning 136
 product analysis 60–1
 product comparison 71
 product disassembly 62–3
 purpose 136
 user trials 70–1
resources 112
risk assessments, health and safety 88–9

S

safety *see* health and safety
safety label 39
sampling 105
satin weave 24, 25
seams
 making 106–7
 neatening 107–8
shape/style development 146–7
shaping techniques 108–9

sharps 95
sketched ideas, design 140–1
slow clothes 79
smart fabrics 32, 32–3
social influences 72–5
specifications
 design 64–5, 139
 fabric specification 36–7
 manufacturing specification 64–5, 114–15
 product specification 64–5, 115
testing/evaluating 168–9
spray diffuser 95
spreadsheet 116
squeegee 95
staple 10
stitching by machine 98–9
style/shape development 146–7
surface decoration, fabric enhancement 44
sustainability 82–3
sustainable 20
synthetic fabrics 14–17
synthetic fibres 14, 14–17
 properties 15–17
system 101

T

tally chart 71
target market 57, 75
task analysis 57
technique 45
Tencel 84–5
 testing/evaluating 166–71
 consumers 168–9
 design ideas 68–9
 design specifications 64–5
 final evaluation reports 170–1
 specifications 168–9
textile components 50–1
textile products, making 160–1
toile 103
trade name 14
traditional costume 75
trend forecasts 56–7
twill weave 24, 25

U

user trials 70–1
UV protection 87

W

warp knit 28, 29
wearable electronics 72–4, 73
weft knit 28
weight 24, 25
working drawings 114
workstations 101
woven fabrics 24–5, 25

Y

yarn 10